INSTANT
Spanish
Vocabulary Builder
with Online Audio

INSTANT
Spanish
Vocabulary Builder
with Online Audio

TOM MEANS, PH.D.

HIPPOCRENE BOOKS, INC.
NEW YORK

Audio files available at www.hippocrenebooks.com

Online audio edition, 2018.
Text copyright © 2003 Tom Means
Audio copyright © 2003 Hippocrene Books, Inc.

Book design by Acme Klong Design.

For information, address:
HIPPOCRENE BOOKS, INC.
171 Madison Avenue
New York, NY 10016
www.hippocrenebooks.com

Previous edition ISBN: 978-0-7818-0981-8

Cataloging-in-publication data available from the Library of Congress.

ISBN 978-0-7818-1374-7

CONTENTS

Audio files available for download at:
http://www.hippocrenebooks.com/instant-spanish-vocabulary-builder.html

*excluding words ending in "–ical," which is a separate Chapter
**excluding words ending in "–ment," which is a separate Chapter

ACKNOWLEDGMENTS

I would like to give special thanks to Juan Pablo Lombana, whose research and bilingual expertise helped make this book possible.

Many thanks to Angelica Bender for her technical assistance with the entire series. Thanks to Ernest Valdés, Enid Bender, Diana Murgio, Dr. Karen Sanchez, John Carleo, and all of my students at Kenneth Cole Productions. Thanks to my editor, Anne Kemper, for her steady and enthusiastic guidance, and also to my former editor, Caroline Gates.

Finally, thanks to all the foreign language teachers who have clearly demonstrated many of these patterns in the past, especially Margarita Madrigal and Michel Thomas.

HOW WE LEARN LANGUAGES

Learning languages is at once a simple yet complex process. It's simple because in essence, we really only need to hear and see a language in order to learn it. If we hear and see a language often enough in contexts that are meaningful to us, we will eventually begin speaking and writing it.

It's complex because the human brain needs to see and hear the language for hundreds and hundreds of hours before it can start to make sense of its patterns and rules. If you can watch/read/listen to the new language enough times, then you can learn it. The ways in which you're exposed to a new language, however, must be meaningful to you in order to be memorable and impact your learning.

So it's complex but not impossible—just find speakers, books, videos, games, music, etc. in the new language and watch/play/read/listen to these resources every day. If the sources you use are memorable and meaningful to you and you have prolonged exposure to them, then after hundreds of hours spent with the new language, your brain will tell your mouth what to do, and abracadabra (!) you will be speaking this new language for the rest of your life.

There are only four ways to become exposed to a new language, so you don't have to worry about how to get started or how to continue toward your goal. The four modalities of language learning are READING, SPEAKING, LISTENING, and WRITING. This book and audio program provide some practice with all four modalities.

In order to learn a language, the first steps and most impactful modalities are LISTENING and READING. These allow learners to collect information (the other two modalities, speaking and writing, are aimed at producing the language once you get some "gas" in the tank). I strongly recommend watching television or movies in the new language. Here's the most important part: You will not understand everything you hear (sometimes it will feel like you don't understand anything!) but your brain will be making sense of all this valuable information so that it can eventually comprehend it and produce it. Try to find a TV program and dozens of movies that interest you in the new language. Watch them with a regular routine, even if it's only thirty minutes per day. And most importantly, keep watching and listening when you don't understand what they're saying! Your brain will make sense of it all but it needs the "nutrition" of hundreds of hours of input to make sense of it. Feed your brain the new language every day.

This book/online audio program provides obvious examples for listening and reading—read the words out loud in each chapter and listen to the examples and stories in each chapter. The reason I emphasize listening and reading first is because that's how we all learned our first language. Babies don't speak or write in their language until they've heard it and seen it for several years. This is very similar to what your brain needs for your new language. There are some differences between how a baby learns a first language and how children and adults learn second/third languages, but the fundamental requirement of hearing and seeing the language in abundance is the same for both.

The other two modalities are also important: you need to practice SPEAKING and WRITING in the new language in order to develop advanced levels of communication. This book/online audio program provides opportunities to practice writing and speaking—especially in the four exercises that end each of the chapters. You will be challenged to match words and to write simple sentences about the stories. For speaking, you should imitate the native speaker as he/she pronounces the words and expressions in every chapter (they are all set in **bold**), and you can also read the stories out loud to practice your pronunciation.

Lastly, I want to emphasize the importance of patience. Your brain can learn any language and it will do it very gradually. You only need to do four things, as summarized here:

- **Listen to/watch the language in material that interests you.** Keep watching even when you don't understand everything. After hundreds of hours of this, your brain will reward your efforts with understanding.

INSTANT Spanish Vocabulary Builder

- **Read the language in material that interests you.** This can be anything that is written in the language: song lyrics, cartoons, illustrated books, magazines, websites, word games, etc. Keep reading because this will also help your ears eventually understand the listening task better.

- **Speak the language and make sure that what you are saying is important to you.** Practice speaking with a real person about your life, your family, your goals, your challenges. As you speak to someone, they will naturally respond and then you will also be working on your listening. Even if you can't find a conversation partner right now, imitate how people speak—when you are home, you can imitate people from videos and online speech.

- **Write the language and make sure you are writing about things that are authentic.** For example, try to write a description of your daily routine, your family, your residence, etc. If possible, find someone to provide you with some instruction. It does not have to be formal instruction but you will need some guidance.

For more information on these tips, please watch some videos on my YouTube channel, "Professor JT Means." If you have discipline, patience and interest in the new language (and you follow these steps) progress is inevitable.

INTRODUCTION

Instant **Spanish Vocabulary Builder** can add thousands of words to your Spanish vocabulary. It is designed to be a supplement for students of Spanish at all levels. This book will help a student to learn to communicate effectively by dramatically increasing his/her Spanish vocabulary.

There are thousands of English words that are connected to their Spanish counterparts by word-ending patterns. This guide will illustrate those patterns and demonstrate how easily they work. The simple reason is that most of Spanish and much of English is derived from Latin. This means that the two languages share a large number of root words, which makes vocabulary building much easier.

Vocabulary building is one of the keys for successful language learning. This book presents vocabulary patterns between English and Spanish in such a systematic fashion that expanding your vocabulary will be easy and enjoyable. I believe it is the only one of its kind.

Instant Spanish Vocabulary Builder is very easy to use. The 24 patterns presented in this book are based on word-endings (suffixes) and the chapters are listed alphabetically. For example, the first chapter presents English words that end in "–al" (capital, normal, etc.) Many of these words end in "–al" in Spanish also (capital, normal, etc.)

The second chapter presents English words that end in "–ance" (distance, importance, etc.) Many of these words correspond to "–ancia" in Spanish (distancia, importancia, etc.) In most cases, you only need to slightly change the ending of the English word to arrive at the correct Spanish word. These words are commonly referred to as cognates: words related by common derivation or descent.

AUDIO ACCOMPANIMENT: This book comes with online audio accompaniment which is available for free download. Every chapter contains many recorded words that typify how words under that pattern are pronounced—all words **in bold** are on the recording. After each Spanish word there will be a pause—it is important for the reader to imitate the native speaker during that pause.

Every chapter also contains common phrases and expressions that are recorded on the audio accompaniment. After every recorded expression there will be a pause for the reader to imitate the native speaker. All expressions **in bold** are on the recording.

In the exercise section of each chapter there are stories for the student to read and listen to with questions that follow. These stories are **in bold** and are also on the recording. They are read by a native speaker at standard speed. Readers are not expected to understand every word of each story, but it is important for language learners to hear new vocabulary words used in an authentic context by a native speaker.

EXERCISES: At the end of every chapter, there are exercises for the reader to do. The first exercise is a matching exercise that reinforces the new words learned in the chapter. The second exercise is a story followed by questions. Every chapter contains a short story about Juan and Angélica, two young Spaniards traveling through Spain.

ANSWER KEY: Answers for the exercises are available in the Answer Key section.

INSTANT Spanish Vocabulary Builder

"FALSE FRIENDS":
Sometimes the English word and the Spanish word will look alike and sound alike, but have different meanings. These are often referred to as "false friends" or "false cognates." When this is the case, a more appropriate definition will be provided alongside the translation. One such example can be seen with the English word "parent."

ENGLISH . . . . SPANISH
parent . . . . pariente (meaning "a relative")

In some rare cases, the English and Spanish word possess such different meanings that the pair was not included in this book. For example, the meaning of the English word "journal" has no relation to the meaning of the Spanish word jornal (day's pay). In other rare cases, overly technical words were not included in this book.

DEVIATIONS IN SPELLING:
Precise spelling of the Spanish words may differ from the English words in more ways than just the endings. If you are interested in spelling the word correctly, please pay close attention to the Spanish column. For example,

ENGLISH . . . . SPANISH
dictionary . . . . diccionario

PRONUNCIATION GUIDE:

All bolded words in this brief pronunciation guide are recorded on the accompanying audio, **track 25.**

There are 27 letters in the Spanish alphabet (one more than in the English alphabet). The additional letter is "ñ." Listed below is a brief guide to Spanish pronunciation. English equivalent sounds have been provided whenever possible.

Spanish vowel	Example	Approximate English sound
A	**España**	ah
E	**excelente**	eh
I	**día**	ee
O	**loco**	oh
U	**mucho**	oooh

There are a few pairings that produce distinct sounds that we will go over next:

"ce" and "ci" always produce a soft sound like the English letter "s": **cena** (dinner); **cita** (appointment)

The pairing "ge" produces a soft sound similar to the word "head": **gente** (people)
The pairing "gi" produces a sound similar to the word "he": **giro** (turn)

"ca" produces a hard sound similar to the word "car": **casa** (house)
"co" sounds approximately like the beginning of "colon": **código** (code)
"cu" produces a hard sound similar to the word "cool": **cubo** (bucket)

"ga" sounds approximately like the beginning of "garbage": **ganar** (to win/to earn)

"go" produces a hard sound similar to the word "going": **gota** (drop)

"gu" produces a hard sound similar to the word "guru": **gula** (gluttony)

"gui" sounds approximately like the word "gear": **guitarra** (guitar)

"gue" produces a hard sound similar to the word "ghetto": **guerrero** (warrior)

The "cc" pairing usually produces a sound similar to "x" in the word "ax": **acción** (action)

The "je" pairing sounds similar to the word "hedge": **jefe** (boss)

The "ll" sounds like the "ll" in "tortilla": **pasillo** (hallway)

The "ñ" sounds like the "ny" in "canyon": **años** (years)

Lastly, the letter "h" is silent in Spanish: **hasta** (until)

IMPORTANT NOTE ON GENDER: Unless otherwise noted in the chapter introduction, all Spanish nouns and adjectives listed in this book are in the singular, masculine form. All nouns are listed without the article that typically accompanies them.

WORKS CONSULTED

Larousse Diccionario Español-Ingles, Ingles-Español. Primera Edicion. México D.F., México: Larousse, 1999.

Merriam-Webster's Collegiate Dictionary, Tenth Edition. Springfield, MA: Merriam-Webster, 2000.

Vox, Diccionario General de la Lengua Española (CD-ROM). Barcelona, Spain: Bibliograf, 1997.

Devney, Dorothy M. Guide to Spanish Suffixes. Chicago: Passport Books, 1992.

Knorre, Marty; Dorwick, Thalia; Perez-Girones, Ana Maria; Glass, William R.; Villareal, Hildebrando. Puntos de Partida, Fifth Edition. Boston: McGraw-Hill, 1997.

Madrigal, Margarita. Margarita's Magical Key to Spanish. New York: Doubleday, 1989.

Prado, Marcial. NTC's Dictionary of Spanish False Cognates. Chicago, NTC Publishing Group, 1993.

Thomas, Michel. Spanish with Michel Thomas. Chicago: NTC Publishing Group, 2000.

A NOTE FROM THE AUTHOR

When I first started studying Spanish, I translated an old trick I had learned from Italian: most English words that end in "–tion" stay the same in Spanish but their ending changes to "–ción." I was soon confidently speaking of the new "situación" that I had seen at the "estación," or about the "condición" of this or that. I was convinced that I had found the "solución" to speaking Spanish!

I know that this vocabulary bridge aided my Spanish skills greatly and fed my enthusiasm for learning and using a beautiful language.

In this book I have collected the 24 most common and applicable vocabulary bridges that exist between English and Spanish. I have done this in the hope that readers find the same immediate application that I did early in my language studies. I hope you find them useful.

A NOTE TO THE USER

The focus of this book is on vocabulary development. However, as with all effective language materials, the vocabulary has been set in an authentic cultural context with realistic characters and stories to encourage immediate applicability in real-life situations.

The exercises are suitable for individual and group work. Teachers will find that the 24 chapters easily can be incorporated into a one-year curriculum.

-al /-al

Many English words ending in "–al" have the same ending in Spanish (excluding words ending in "–ical," which is a separate pattern).

Spanish words ending in "–al" are usually adjectives or nouns. For example,

artificial (adj.) = *artificial*
animal (n.) = *un animal*

ENGLISH. . . . . . . SPANISH	

All words and phrases in **bold** *are on* **Track 1** *of the accompanying audio.*

abdominal	abdominal
abnormal	anormal
accidental.	accidental
actual.	actual *(meaning "current, present")*
additional.	adicional
adverbial	adverbial
amoral	amoral
ancestral	ancestral
animal	**animal**
"It's an animal!"	**"¡Es un animal!"**
annual	anual
antiliberal.	antiliberal
antisocial	antisocial
arsenal.	arsenal
artificial	artificial
asexual	asexual
asocial.	asocial
audiovisual.	audiovisual
autumnal	otoñal

banal . . . . banal
baptismal . . . . bautismal
beneficial . . . . beneficial *(more commonly "beneficioso")*

bestial . . . . bestial
biannual . . . . bianual
biennial . . . . bienal
bifocal . . . . bifocal
bilateral . . . . bilateral
bisexual . . . . bisexual
bronchial . . . . bronquial
brutal . . . . **brutal**
   "It's a brutal reaction." . . . . . . **"Es una reacción brutal"**.

canal . . . . canal *(also used for "TV channel")*
cannibal . . . . caníbal
capital . . . . **capital** *(for geography, use "la capital"; for finance, use "el capital")*

cardinal . . . . cardinal
carnal . . . . carnal
carnival . . . . carnaval *(also used for period of Mardi Gras)*

casual . . . . casual *(also used for "by chance")*
cathedral . . . . catedral
causal . . . . causal
celestial . . . . celestial
central . . . . **central**
cereal . . . . cereal
cerebral . . . . cerebral
ceremonial . . . . ceremonial
choral . . . . coral
circumstantial . . . . circunstancial
coincidental . . . . coincidencial
collateral . . . . colateral
colloquial . . . . coloquial
colonial . . . . colonial

colossal . . . . colosal
commercial. . . . . comercial
communal. . . . . comunal
conceptual . . . . conceptual
conditional . . . . condicional
confessional . . . . confesional *(only an adjective)*
confidential. . . . . confidencial
confrontational . . . . confrontacional
constitutional. . . . . constitucional
contextual. . . . . contextual
continental . . . . **continental**
contractual . . . . contractual
controversial . . . . controversial
conventional . . . . convencional
conversational. . . . . conversacional
coral . . . . coral
cordial . . . . cordial
corporal . . . . corporal
corral. . . . . corral
correctional . . . . correccional
cranial . . . . craneal
credential . . . . credencial
criminal . . . . criminal
crucial . . . . **crucial**
   "Tomorrow is a crucial day." . . . . **"Mañana es un día crucial"**.
crystal . . . . cristal
cultural. . . . . cultural

decimal . . . . decimal
dental . . . . dental
departmental. . . . . departamental
devotional . . . . devocional
diagonal. . . . . **diagonal**
dictatorial. . . . . dictatorial
differential . . . . diferencial
digital . . . . digital

dimensional . . . . dimensional
disloyal . . . . desleal
divisional . . . . divisional
doctoral . . . . doctoral
dorsal . . . . dorsal
dual . . . . dual
ducal . . . . ducal
dysfunctional . . . . disfuncional

editorial . . . . editorial
electoral . . . . electoral
elemental . . . . elemental *(meaning "elementary")*
emotional . . . . emocional
episcopal . . . . episcopal
equal . . . . **igual**
equatorial . . . . ecuatorial
essential . . . . esencial
eternal . . . . eternal *(more commonly "eterno")*
eventual . . . . eventual *(meaning "possible")*
exceptional . . . . excepcional
existential . . . . existencial
experimental . . . . experimental
exponential . . . . exponencial
extramarital . . . . extramatrimonial

facial . . . . facial
factual . . . . factual
fatal . . . . fatal *(also used for "terrible," "lousy")*
federal . . . . federal
festival . . . . festival
fetal . . . . fetal
feudal . . . . feudal
filial . . . . filial
final . . . . **final**
fiscal . . . . fiscal
floral . . . . floral

focal . . . . focal
formal . . . . formal
fraternal . . . . fraternal
frontal . . . . frontal
frugal. . . . . frugal
functional . . . . funcional
fundamental . . . . **fundamental**
funeral . . . . funeral

gastrointestinal . . . . gastrointestinal
general . . . . **general**
generational . . . . generacional
genial . . . . genial *(meaning "talented," "brilliant")*
germinal. . . . . germinal
glacial . . . . glacial
global . . . . global
gradual . . . . gradual
grammatical . . . . gramatical
gravitational . . . . gravitacional
guttural. . . . . gutural

habitual . . . . habitual
heterosexual . . . . heterosexual
homosexual . . . . homosexual
horizontal. . . . . horizontal
hormonal . . . . hormonal
hospital . . . . **hospital**

ideal . . . . **ideal**
illegal. . . . . **ilegal**
    "Stealing is illegal.". . . . . . . **"Robar es ilegal".**
immaterial . . . . inmaterial
immoral . . . . inmoral
immortal. . . . . inmortal
impartial. . . . . imparcial
imperial . . . . imperial

impersonal	impersonal
inaugural	inaugural
incidental	incidental
individual	individual *(adjective only; noun is "individuo")*
industrial	industrial
infernal	infernal
informal	informal
initial	**inicial**
institutional	institucional
instrumental	instrumental
insubstantial	insustancial
integral	integral
intellectual	intelectual
intentional.	intencional
intercontinental	intercontinental
international	**internacional**
"It's an international company."	**"Es una compañía internacional".**
interpersonal.	interpersonal
interracial.	interracial
intestinal.	intestinal
irrational	irracional
jovial	jovial
judicial.	judicial
labial.	labial
lateral	lateral
latitudinal	latitudinal
legal	**legal**
lethal	letal
liberal	liberal
literal	literal

local . . . . local *(also used as "commercial premises")*

longitudinal. . . . . longitudinal

loyal . . . . leal

manual. . . . . manual

marginal. . . . . marginal

marital . . . . marital

martial . . . . marcial

material . . . . material

maternal. . . . . maternal

matriarchal. . . . . matriarcal

matrimonial . . . . matrimonial

medicinal . . . . medicinal

medieval . . . . medieval

menstrual . . . . menstrual

mental . . . . **mental**

    "It's a mental problem." . . . . . **"Es un problema mental".**

meridional . . . . meridional *(meaning "Southern")*

metal . . . . metal

mineral. . . . . mineral

modal . . . . modal

monumental . . . . monumental

moral. . . . . moral

mortal . . . . mortal

multicultural . . . . multicultural

multifunctional. . . . . multifuncional

multinational . . . . multinacional

municipal . . . . municipal

mural. . . . . mural

musical. . . . . musical

mutual . . . . mutual *(more commonly "mutuo")*

nasal . . . . nasal

natal . . . . natal

national . . . . **nacional**
natural . . . . natural
naval . . . . naval
Neanderthal . . . . neandertal
neutral . . . . neutral
nominal . . . . nominal
normal . . . . normal
numeral . . . . numeral
nuptial . . . . nupcial
nutritional . . . . nutricional

occasional . . . . ocasional *(also used for "accidental")*
occidental . . . . occidental *(meaning "Western")*
occupational . . . . ocupacional
octagonal . . . . octagonal
official . . . . oficial
operational . . . . operacional
optional . . . . opcional
oral . . . . oral
ordinal . . . . ordinal
organizational . . . . organizacional
oriental . . . . oriental *(meaning "Eastern")*
original . . . . **original**
ornamental . . . . ornamental
oval . . . . oval

papal . . . . papal
paranormal . . . . paranormal
parochial . . . . parroquial
partial . . . . parcial
pastoral . . . . pastoral
patrimonial . . . . patrimonial
pectoral . . . . pectoral
pedal . . . . pedal
pedestal . . . . pedestal
penal . . . . penal

personal	personal
phenomenal	fenomenal
plural	plural
portal	portal
positional	posicional
postal	postal
postnatal	postnatal
potential	potencial
preferential	preferencial
prenatal	prenatal
prenuptial	prenupcial
prepositional	preposicional
presidential	presidencial
primordial	primordial
principal	**principal**
procedural	procedimental
processional	procesional
professional	profesional
promotional	promocional
proportional	proporcional
proverbial	proverbial
providential	providencial
provincial	provincial
provisional	provisional
punctual	puntual
racial	racial
radial	radial
radical	radical
rational	racional
real	real
recital	recital
regional	**regional**
relational	relacional
residential	residencial
residual	residual

reverential . . . . reverencial
ritual . . . . ritual
rival . . . . rival
royal . . . . real
rural . . . . rural

sacramental . . . . sacramental
sacrificial . . . . sacrificial
sculptural . . . . escultural
semifinal . . . . semifinal
seminal . . . . seminal
senatorial . . . . senatorial
sensational . . . . sensacional
sensual . . . . sensual
sentimental . . . . sentimental
sepulchral . . . . sepulcral
sequential . . . . secuencial
sexual . . . . sexual
signal . . . . señal
social . . . . **social**
sociocultural . . . . sociocultural
spatial . . . . espacial
special . . . . **especial**
spinal . . . . espinal
spiral . . . . espiral
spiritual . . . . espiritual
structural . . . . estructural
subliminal . . . . subliminal
substantial . . . . sustancial
subtotal . . . . subtotal
subtropical . . . . subtropical
superficial . . . . superficial
supernatural . . . . supernatural
surreal . . . . surreal

tangential . . . . tangencial

temperamental . . . . temperamental

temporal. . . . . temporal *(also used for "temporary" and "storm")*

terminal . . . . terminal

territorial . . . . territorial

testimonial . . . . testimonial

textual . . . . textual

thermal. . . . . termal *(meaning "related to springs")*

tonal . . . . tonal

torrential. . . . . torrencial

total. . . . . **total**

traditional. . . . . tradicional

transcendental. . . . . trascendental

transcontinental . . . . transcontinental

transitional . . . . transicional

transsexual . . . . transexual

tribal . . . . tribal

tribunal . . . . tribunal *(meaning "courthouse")*

trivial . . . . trivial

tropical. . . . . **tropical**

unconditional . . . . incondicional

unconstitutional . . . . inconstitucional

unequal . . . . desigual

unilateral . . . . unilateral

universal. . . . . universal

unofficial . . . . extraoficial

unreal . . . . irreal

unusual . . . . inusual

urinal. . . . . orinal

usual . . . . usual

vegetal. . . . . vegetal

venal . . . . venal

verbal . . . . verbal

vertical . . . . vertical

vice-presidential . . . . vicepresidencial

viral . . . . viral

virtual . . . . virtual

visceral . . . . visceral

visual . . . . visual

vital . . . . vital

vocal . . . . vocal *(also a noun, "vowel")*

vocational . . . . vocacional

zonal . . . . zonal

1A.

Match associated words and/or synonyms.

Una las palabras que están relacionadas o que son sinónimos.

1. animal	contrato
2. personal	gato
3. artificial	sintético
4. crucial	perfecto
5. ideal	importante
6. legal	privado
7. final	terminar

1B.

Listen to and read the story. Answer the following questions in complete sentences.

Escuche y lea el cuento. Responda las siguientes preguntas, usando oraciones completas.

(This chapter presents the first story of the travels of Juan and Angélica. Every chapter will feature a new story about these two young Spaniards traveling through Spain. Please listen to and read each story carefully before answering the questions that follow.)

Juan y Angélica son dos jóvenes de Bilbao; ellos quieren hacer un viaje (take a trip)**. Hay un problema—Juan quiere hacer un viaje <u>internacional</u> y Angélica quiere hacer un viaje <u>nacional</u>. Juan dice, "Pero Angélica, tu idea no es <u>original</u>". Angélica dice, "¡Vamos, Juan, no ahora** (not now)**!" Al final, Angélica gana; Juan decide que no es <u>esencial</u> hacer un viaje <u>internacional</u> ahora. Angélica tiene algunas ideas <u>generales</u> para su itinerario. Juan dice, "No quiero visitar a tu tío en**

Córdoba. ¡Él es demasiado <u>formal</u> y <u>tradicional</u>!" Angélica dice, "Veremos...(we'll see)".

1. ¿De dónde son Juan y Angélica?

2. ¿Qué tipo de viaje quiere hacer Juan?

3. ¿Qué tipo de viaje quiere hacer Angélica?

4. ¿Qué dice Juan de la idea de Angélica?

5. ¿Según Juan (according to Juan), cómo es el tío de Angélica?

Chapter 2

Many English words ending in "–ance" correspond to "–ancia" in Spanish.

Spanish words ending in "–ancia" are usually feminine nouns. For example,

distance = *la distancia*

ENGLISH. . . . . . . SPANISH

All words and phrases in **bold** *are on* **Track 2** *of the accompanying audio.*

abundance . . . . abundancia
ambulance . . . . **ambulancia**
arrogance. . . . . **arrogancia**
    "Nobody likes arrogance." . . . **"A nadie le gusta la arrogancia"**.
assistance. . . . . asistencia

circumstance. . . . . circunstancia
clairvoyance. . . . . clarividencia
concordance. . . . . concordancia
consonance . . . . consonancia
constance. . . . . constancia

discordance . . . . discordancia
dissonance . . . . disonancia
distance . . . . **distancia**

elegance. . . . . **elegancia**
extravagance . . . . extravagancia
exuberance. . . . . exuberancia

flagrance . . . . flagrancia

fragrance . . . . fragancia
France . . . . Francia

ignorance. . . . . ignorancia
importance . . . . **importancia**
 "What is the importance?" . . . **"¿Cuál es la importancia?"**
inobservance . . . . inobservancia
insignificance . . . . insignificancia
instance . . . . instancia
intemperance . . . . intemperancia
intolerance . . . . **intolerancia**
irrelevance . . . . irrelevancia

militance . . . . militancia

observance. . . . . observancia

perseverance . . . . **perseverancia**
 "Perseverance is important." . . . **"La perseverancia es importante".**
predominance. . . . . predominancia
preponderance . . . . preponderancia
protuberance . . . . protuberancia

redundance . . . . redundancia
relevance . . . . relevancia
repugnance . . . . repugnancia
resistance . . . . resistencia
resonance. . . . . resonancia

substance . . . . **substancia**

temperance. . . . . temperancia
tolerance . . . . **tolerancia**

variance. . . . . variancia
vigilance . . . . vigilancia

2A.

Una las palabras que están relacionadas o que son sinónimos.

1. fragancia	hospital
2. distancia	significado
3. perseverancia	soberbia
4. tolerancia	lejos
5. arrogancia	constancia
6. ambulancia	perfume
7. importancia	paciencia

2B.

Escuche y lea el cuento. Responda las siguientes preguntas, usando oraciones completas.

Para organizar su viaje, Juan y Angélica hablan de muchas cosas. Juan habla de la <u>importancia</u> de no gastar (spend) **mucho; de hecho, Juan no tiene mucha <u>tolerancia</u> hacia el mundo "chic". El sabe que hay gran <u>distancia</u> que cubrir, y que la <u>perseverancia</u> será necesaria. Angélica también entiende la <u>importancia</u> de no gastar mucho dinero durante el viaje. Ella pide** (asks for) **solamente una cosa: quiere ver un baile profesional** (a professional dance) **en Valencia. Una amiga le dijo que es un espectáculo de una <u>elegancia</u> increíble. Juan dice, "Veremos...".**

1. ¿Juan habla de la importancia de qué cosa?

2. ¿Juan no tiene mucha tolerancia hacia qué?

3. ¿Qué será necesario?

4. ¿ Angélica entiende la importancia de no gastar mucho dinero?

5. ¿Cómo responde Juan al pedido (request) de Angélica?

English words ending in "–ant" generally correspond to "–ante" in Spanish.

Spanish words ending in "–ante" are usually adjectives or nouns. For example,

> arrogant (adj.) = *arrogante*
> deodorant (n.) = *el desodorante*

ENGLISH. . . . . . . SPANISH

All words and phrases in **bold** *are on* **Track 3** *of the accompanying audio.*

aberrant . . . . aberrante
abundant . . . . **abundante**
ambulant . . . . ambulante
antioxidant . . . . antioxidante
arrogant . . . . **arrogante**
   "He is very arrogant." . . . . . . **"El es muy arrogante".**
aspirant . . . . aspirante
assailant . . . . asaltante

brilliant . . . . brillante

colorant . . . . colorante
commandant . . . . comandante
communicant . . . . comunicante
concordant . . . . concordante
consonant . . . . consonante
constant . . . . **constante** *(also used for "consistent")*
consultant . . . . consultante
contaminant . . . . contaminante

debutant . . . . debutante

deodorant.	**desodorante**
determinant	determinante
discordant	discordante
disinfectant	desinfectante
dissonant	disonante
distant	distante
dominant	dominante

elegant.	**elegante**
elephant.	**elefante**
emigrant.	emigrante
entrant	entrante
equidistant	equidistante
errant.	errante
exorbitant.	exorbitante
expectant	expectante
extravagant	extravagante *(also used for "odd")*
exuberant.	exuberante
exultant	exultante

flagellant	flagelante
flagrant	flagrante
fluctuant.	fluctuante
fumigant.	fumigante

gallant	galante
giant	gigante

ignorant.	**ignorante**

"What an ignorant question!" . . **"¡Qué pregunta tan ignorante!"**

immigrant.	**inmigrante**
implant.	implante
important	**importante**
incessant	incesante
inconstant.	inconstante
indignant	indignante

infant . . . . infante
informant . . . . informante
inhabitant . . . . habitante
inobservant . . . . inobservante
insignificant . . . . insignificante
instant . . . . **instante**
intolerant . . . . intolerante
irrelevant . . . . irrelevante
irritant . . . . irritante
itinerant . . . . itinerante

lubricant . . . . lubricante

merchant . . . . mercante *(only used as an adjective)*
migrant . . . . emigrante
militant . . . . militante
mutant . . . . mutante

observant . . . . observante *(more commonly*
                                                   "observador")
occupant . . . . **ocupante**
operant . . . . operante

palpitant . . . . palpitante
participant . . . . **participante**
pedant . . . . pedante
piquant . . . . picante
predominant . . . . predominante
preponderant . . . . preponderante
Protestant . . . . protestante

radiant . . . . radiante
rampant . . . . rampante
recalcitrant . . . . recalcitrante
redundant . . . . redundante
refrigerant . . . . refrigerante

relaxant	relajante
relevant	relevante
repugnant	repugnante
resonant	resonante
restaurant	**restaurante**

"That restaurant is cheap." . . . **"Ese restaurante es barato".**

stimulant	**estimulante** *(also used for "stimulating")*
supplicant	suplicante

tolerant	tolerante
transplant	transplante
triumphant	**triunfante**

vacant	vacante
variant	variante
vibrant	vibrante
vigilant	vigilante

3A.

Una las palabras que están relacionadas o que son sinónimos.

1. ignorante	evidente
2. elegante	animal
3. importante	pretencioso
4. elefante	cafetería
5. arrogante	esencial
6. flagrante	desconocedor
7. restaurante	fino

3B.

Escuche y lea el cuento. Responda las siguientes preguntas, usando oraciones completas.

Juan y Angélica deciden ir primero a una ciudad <u>importante</u>: ¡Barcelona! Angélica dice, "Pero Juan, ¿es verdad que la gente** (the people) **de Barcelona es <u>arrogante</u>?"** Juan responde, **"¡Pero qué pregunta tan <u>ignorante</u>! No, la gente de Barcelona no es <u>arrogante</u>, su modo de vestir** (way of dressing) **es muy <u>elegante</u> y saben que la historia de Barcelona es muy <u>importante</u>, pero... son personas muy simpáticas".** **Juan tiene un amigo, Andrés, que vive en Barcelona y tiene un <u>restaurante</u> que se llama El <u>Elefante</u> Rojo. Apenas llegan** (as soon as they arrive) **a Barcelona, van a comer al <u>restaurante</u> de Andrés. El les sirve una cena <u>abundante</u>.**

1. ¿A qué ciudad van Juan y Angélica?

2. ¿Qué piensa Angélica de la gente de Barcelona?

3. ¿Qué dice Juan del modo de vestir de la gente de Barcelona?

4. ¿Cómo describe Juan la historia de Barcelona?

5. ¿Cómo se llama el restaurante de Andrés?

-ar/-ar

Many English words ending in "–ar" have the same ending in Spanish.

Spanish words ending in "–ar" are usually verbs, nouns, or adjectives. For example,

> to arrive (v.) = *llegar*   a dollar *(n.)* = *un dólar*
> spectacular (adj.) = *espectacular*

ENGLISH. . . . . . . SPANISH

All words and phrases in **bold** *are on* **Track 4** *of the accompanying audio.*

altar. . . . . altar

angular . . . . angular

antinuclear . . . . antinuclear

bipolar. . . . . bipolar

Caesar. . . . . César

cardiovascular . . . . cardiovascular

caviar . . . . caviar

cellular. . . . . **celular**

    "It's a cellular phone." . . . . . . **"Es un teléfono celular"**.

circular. . . . . **circular**

    "It has a circular shape." . . . . **"Tiene una forma circular"**.

collar . . . . collar *(meaning "necklace")*

curricular . . . . curricular

dollar. . . . . dólar

electronuclear . . . . electronuclear

exemplar . . . . ejemplar

extracurricular. . . . . extracurricular

familiar . . . . familiar

glandular . . . . glandular
globular . . . . globular
granular. . . . . granular

insular . . . . insular
intramuscular . . . . intramuscular
irregular. . . . . irregular

jugular . . . . yugular

lunar . . . . lunar *(also used for "mole")*

modular . . . . modular
molecular . . . . molecular
multicellular . . . . multicelular
muscular. . . . . muscular *(only used for "of the muscle")*

nectar . . . . néctar
nuclear. . . . . nuclear
    "Nuclear war is terrible.". . . . **"La guerra nuclear es terrible".**

ocular . . . . ocular

particular . . . . particular
peculiar . . . . peculiar
peninsular. . . . . peninsular
perpendicular . . . . perpendicular
polar . . . . **polar**
popular . . . . **popular** *(also used for "of the people")*

radar. . . . . radar
rectangular. . . . . rectangular
regular. . . . . regular *(also used for "less than good")*

scholar . . . . escolar *(meaning "pupil,"*
or "of the school")

secular . . . . secular
semicircular . . . . semicircular
similar . . . . similar
singular . . . . singular
solar . . . . solar
spectacular . . . . **espectacular**
stellar . . . . estelar
subpolar . . . . subpolar
sugar . . . . azúcar

thermonuclear . . . . termonuclear
triangular . . . . triangular
tubular . . . . tubular
tzar . . . . zar

unicellular . . . . unicelular
unpopular . . . . impopular

vascular . . . . vascular
vehicular . . . . vehicular
vulgar . . . . **vulgar**

Una las palabras que están relacionadas o que son sinónimos.

1. cardiovascular	corazón
2. regular	moneda
3. singular	atómico
4. circular	parecido
5. similar	redondo
6. dólar	constante
7. nuclear	único

4B.

Escuche y lea el cuento. Responda las siguientes preguntas, usando oraciones completas.

Mientras están en (while in) **Barcelona, Juan y Angélica van a una lección de italiano con Andrés, el amigo de Juan. Angélica pregunta, "¿Por qué tienes un interés tan <u>particular</u> por el italiano?" Andrés responde, "Porque el italiano es muy <u>popular</u> en Ibiza, y quiero trabajar** (I want to work) **en Ibiza". Durante la lección, el profesor habla de muchos verbos <u>irregulares</u>. Después de la lección, los tres amigos hablan de la diferencia entre** (between) **el <u>singular</u> y el plural en el italiano. El italiano es muy difícil para Angélica. Ella dice, "¡Nada es <u>regular</u>, todo es <u>irregular</u>! ¡Para mí, el italiano es muy difícil!"**

1. ¿Adónde van mientras están en Barcelona?

2. ¿Por qué estudia Andrés italiano?

3. ¿De qué habla el profesor?

4. ¿Los tres amigos hablan de la diferencia entre qué cosas?

5. ¿Angélica piensa que el italiano es muy regular?

INSTANT Spanish Vocabulary Builder

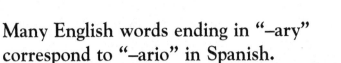

Chapter 5

Many English words ending in "–ary" correspond to "–ario" in Spanish.

Spanish words ending in "–ario" are usually masculine nouns or adjectives. For example,

> anniversary (n.) = *un aniversario*
> ordinary (adj.) = *ordinario*

ENGLISH....... SPANISH

All words and phrases in **bold** *are on* **Track 5** *of the accompanying audio.*

actuary . . . . actuario
adversary. . . . . adversario
anniversary . . . . **aniversario**
antiquary . . . . anticuario
arbitrary. . . . . arbitrario

beneficiary . . . . beneficiario
bestiary . . . . bestiario
binary . . . . binario
breviary . . . . breviario

canary . . . . canario
centenary . . . . centenario
commentary . . . . comentario *(also used for "comment")*
commissary. . . . . comisario
complementary . . . . complementario
contrary . . . . **contrario**
corollary. . . . . corolario
coronary . . . . coronario
culinary . . . . culinario

depository . . . . depositario

diary . . . . diario *(also used for "newspaper")*

dictionary . . . . **diccionario**

    "He is using the dictionary.". . . **"Él está usando el diccionario"**.

dignitary . . . . dignatario

disciplinary . . . . disciplinario

dispensary . . . . dispensario

divisionary . . . . divisionario

documentary . . . . documentario *(more commonly "documental," as a noun)*

emissary . . . . emisario

estuary . . . . estuario

extraordinary . . . . **extraordinario**

fiduciary . . . . fiduciario

fragmentary . . . . fragmentario

functionary . . . . funcionario

funerary . . . . funerario

glossary . . . . **glosario**

hereditary . . . . hereditario

honorary . . . . honorario

imaginary . . . . **imaginario**

    "He has an imaginary friend." . . . **"Él tiene un amigo imaginario"**.

incendiary . . . . incendiario

interdisciplinary . . . . interdisciplinario

intermediary . . . . intermediario

involuntary . . . . involuntario

itinerary . . . . **itinerario**

lapidary . . . . lapidario

legendary . . . . legendario

literary . . . . literario

INSTANT Spanish Vocabulary Builder

mercenary . . . . mercenario
monetary . . . . monetario

necessary . . . . **necesario**
notary . . . . notario

obituary . . . . obituario
ordinary . . . . **ordinario**
ovary . . . . ovario

parliamentary . . . . parlamentario
penitentiary . . . . penitenciario
planetary . . . . planetario
plenary . . . . plenario
primary . . . . primario
proprietary . . . . propietario *(also used for "owner")*

questionary . . . . cuestionario *(meaning "questionnaire")*

reactionary . . . . reaccionario
revolutionary . . . . **revolucionario**
rosary . . . . rosario
rudimentary . . . . rudimentario

salary . . . . **salario**
   "You have a good salary." . . . **"Tu tienes un buen salario"**.
sanctuary . . . . santuario
sanitary . . . . sanitario
secondary . . . . secundario
secretary . . . . **secretario** *(more commonly used in*
                                       feminine form, "secretaria")
sedentary . . . . sedentario
sedimentary . . . . sedimentario
seminary . . . . seminario
solitary . . . . **solitario**
stationary . . . . estacionario

subsidiary. . . . . subsidiario
summary . . . . sumario
supplementary. . . . . suplementario

temporary. . . . . temporario
tertiary. . . . . terciario
tributary . . . . tributario

unitary . . . . unitario
unnecessary . . . . innecesario
urinary. . . . . urinario

veterinary. . . . . veterinario
visionary . . . . visionario
vocabulary . . . . **vocabulario** *(also used for "dictionary")*
   "Vocabulary is important." . . . **"El vocabulario es importante".**
voluntary . . . . voluntario *(also used for "volunteer")*

5A.

Una las palabras que están relacionadas o que son sinónimos.

1.	aniversario	palabras
2.	salario	ruta
3.	necesario	común
4.	vocabulario	cumpleaños
5.	itinerario	opuesto
6.	ordinario	vital
7.	contrario	dinero

5B.

Escuche y lea el cuento. Responda las siguientes preguntas, usando oraciones completas.

Juan y Angélica tienen un <u>itinerario</u> muy intenso en Barcelona. Para no olvidar (to not forget) **su aventura, Angélica quiere comprar un <u>diario</u> para escribir todo. Un día van a las Ramblas, otro día van a la Sagrada Familia, otro día van a Montserrat. Juan dice, "¡Este ritmo** (this pace) **es <u>extraordinario</u>!" Cada noche, Angélica escribe mucho en su <u>diario</u>, pero Juan no comprende. El dice, "No es <u>necesario</u> escribir cada detalle** (every detail)**—¡no es un <u>diccionario</u>!" Angélica responde, "Al <u>contrario</u>, ¡es muy importante escribir cada detalle!"**

1. ¿Cómo es el itinerario de Juan y Angélica en Barcelona?

2. ¿Qué quiere comprar Angélica?

3. ¿Qué escribe Angélica en su diario?

4. ¿Qué dice Juan del ritmo?

5. ¿Según Juan, no es necesario hacer qué cosa?

-ble/-ble

Many English words ending in "–ble" have the same ending in Spanish.

Spanish words ending in "–ble" are usually adjectives. For example,

a <u>flexible</u> schedule = *un horario <u>flexible</u>*

ENGLISH. . . . . . . SPANISH	

All words and phrases in **bold** *are on* **Track 6** *of the accompanying audio.*

abominable	abominable
acceptable	**aceptable**
accessible.	accesible *(also used for "approachable")*
accusable.	acusable
adaptable.	adaptable
adjustable.	ajustable
admirable.	admirable
admissible	admisible
adoptable.	adoptable
adorable	**adorable**
"The baby is adorable."	**"El bebé es adorable".**
affable	afable
agreeable.	agradable
alienable	alienable
alterable.	alterable
amiable	amable
amicable	amigable
appealable.	apelable
applicable	aplicable
appreciable	apreciable
arable	arable
audible	audible

biodegradable . . . . biodegradable

cable . . . . cable
calculable . . . . calculable
cancelable . . . . cancelable
censurable . . . . censurable
classifiable . . . . clasificable
coercible . . . . coercible
collectible . . . . coleccionable
combinable . . . . combinable
combustible . . . . combustible
comfortable . . . . confortable *(more commonly "cómodo")*
commemorable . . . . conmemorable
commensurable . . . . conmensurable
communicable . . . . comunicable
commutable . . . . conmutable
comparable . . . . **comparable**
compatible . . . . compatible
comprehensible . . . . comprensible
computable . . . . computable
condemnable . . . . condenable
condensable . . . . condensable
condonable . . . . condonable
confessable . . . . confesable
conservable . . . . conservable
considerable . . . . considerable
consolable . . . . consolable
consumable . . . . consumible
contestable . . . . contestable
controllable . . . . controlable
controvertible . . . . controvertible
convertible . . . . convertible
corruptible . . . . corruptible
countable . . . . contable (also used for "accountant")
credible . . . . **creíble**
　　　"His story is not credible." . . . **"Su cuento no es creíble".**

criticizable	criticable
culpable	culpable
curable	curable
deductible	deducible
defensible	defendible
definable	definible
degradable	degradable
delectable	deleitable
demonstrable	demostrable
deplorable	deplorable
describable	descriptible
desirable	deseable
destructible	destructible
determinable	determinable
detestable	detestable
digestible	digerible
discussible	discutible
disposable	disponible *(meaning "available")*
disputable	disputable
distillable	destilable
divisible	**divisible**
dubitable	dudable
durable	durable *(more commonly "duradero")*
eligible	elegible
eliminable	eliminable
emendable	enmendable
enviable	envidiable
estimable	estimable
evaporable	evaporable
evitable	evitable
excitable	excitable
excludible	excluible
excusable	**excusable**
expansible	expansible

explicable . . . . explicable
explorable . . . . explorable
exportable . . . . exportable
extensible . . . . extensible

fallible . . . . falible
favorable . . . . favorable
fermentable . . . . fermentable
filmable . . . . filmable
flexible . . . . **flexible**
formidable . . . . formidable *(also used for "great,"*
                                                         "super")

governable . . . . gobernable

habitable . . . . habitable
honorable . . . . honorable
horrible . . . . **horrible**

identifiable . . . . identificable
ignoble . . . . innoble
illegible . . . . ilegible
imaginable . . . . imaginable
imitable . . . . imitable
impassible . . . . impasible
impeccable . . . . **impecable**
"Your Spanish is impeccable." . . . **"Tu español es impecable".**
impenetrable . . . . impenetrable
imperceptible . . . . imperceptible
impermeable . . . . impermeable *(also used for "raincoat")*
imperturbable . . . . imperturbable
implacable . . . . implacable
impossible . . . . **imposible**
impressionable . . . . impresionable
improbable . . . . **improbable**
inaccessible . . . . inaccesible

malleable . . . . maleable

manageable . . . . manejable

maneuverable . . . . maniobrable

measurable . . . . mensurable

memorable . . . . memorable

miserable . . . . **miserable** *(also used for "greedy,"*
or "evil")

modifiable . . . . modificable

multipliable . . . . multiplicable

navigable . . . . navegable

negotiable . . . . negociable

noble . . . . **noble**

notable . . . . notable

observable . . . . observable

operable . . . . operable

ostensible . . . . ostensible

palpable . . . . palpable

pardonable . . . . perdonable

passable . . . . **pasable**

    "The wine is passable (so-so)." . . . **"El vino está pasable nada más"**.

payable . . . . pagable

penetrable . . . . penetrable

perceptible . . . . perceptible

perfectible . . . . perfectible

permeable . . . . permeable

permissible . . . . permisible

persuadable . . . . persuasible

placable . . . . aplacable

plausible . . . . plausible

ponderable . . . . ponderable

possible . . . . **posible**

potable . . . . potable

preferable . . . . preferible

presentable	presentable
probable	**probable**
producible	producible
programmable	programable
provable	probable
publishable	publicable
qualifiable	calificable
quantifiable	cuantificable
realizable	realizable
recommendable	recomendable
reconcilable	reconciliable
recyclable	reciclable
reducible	reducible
reformable	reformable
refutable	refutable
renewable	renovable
repairable	**reparable**
repeatable	repetible
replicable	replicable
reprehensible	reprensible
representable	representable
resistible	resistible
respectable	**respetable**

"She's a respectable lady." . . . **"Es una señora respetable".**

responsible	**responsable**
restorable	restaurable
retractable	retractable
reversible	reversible
revocable	revocable
savable	salvable
sensible	sensible *(meaning "sensitive")*
separable	separable
sociable	sociable

INSTANT Spanish Vocabulary Builder

soluble . . . . soluble
stable . . . . **estable** *(only an*
adjective; "horse stable" is "establo")
superable . . . . superable
susceptible . . . . susceptible

tangible . . . . tangible
terminable . . . . terminable
terrible . . . . terrible
tolerable . . . . tolerable
touchable . . . . tocable
transferable . . . . transferible
transformable . . . . transformable

unacceptable . . . . inaceptable
unadaptable . . . . inadaptable
unalterable . . . . inalterable
unclassifiable . . . . inclasificable
uncontrollable . . . . incontrolable
undesirable . . . . indeseable
undeterminable . . . . indeterminable
undisputable . . . . indisputable
unimaginable . . . . inimaginable
unintelligible . . . . ininteligible
unsociable . . . . insociable
unstable . . . . inestable
untouchable . . . . intocable
utilizable . . . . utilizable

variable . . . . **variable**
venerable . . . . venerable
verifiable . . . . verificable
viable . . . . viable
visible . . . . **visible**
vulnerable . . . . vulnerable

6A.

Una las palabras que están relacionadas o que son sinónimos.

1. flexible	rígido
2. terrible	bonito
3. probable	seguro
4. estable	posible
5. inflexible	infeliz
6. miserable	elástico
7. adorable	horrible

6B.

Escuche y lea el cuento. Responda las siguientes preguntas, usando oraciones completas.

Después de unos días en Barcelona, Juan y Angélica toman el tren a Valencia. Durante el viaje en tren tienen una pelea (an argument). **Angélica le dice a Juan, "¡Tú eres muy <u>irresponsable</u>! ¡No reservaste** (you didn't reserve) **los asientos para el baile!" Juan responde, "¡Tú eres <u>inflexible</u>, podemos ir en otra ocasión; es muy <u>probable</u> que regresemos a Valencia algún día!" Angélica dice, "¡Eres <u>imposible</u>! ¡Es bastante <u>improbable</u> que regresemos a Valencia!" Al final Juan pide disculpas** (apologizes) **y dice que será mucho mas <u>responsable</u> durante el resto del viaje. Angélica pregunta si será <u>posible</u> comprar los boletos para el baile en Valencia. Juan responde, "Veremos...".**

1. ¿Adónde van después de Barcelona?

2. ¿Qué piensa Angélica de Juan?

3. ¿Qué dice Juan de Angélica?

4. ¿Angélica piensa que es probable que regresen a Valencia algún día?

5. ¿Qué pregunta Angélica al final?

-ct/-cto

English words ending in "–ct" often correspond to "–cto" in Spanish.

Spanish words ending in "–cto" are usually masculine nouns or adjectives. For example,

> contact (n.) = *un contacto*
> direct (adj.) = *directo*

ENGLISH. . . . . . . SPANISH	

All words and phrases in **bold** *are on* **Track 7** *of the accompanying audio.*

abstract . . . . abstracto

act. . . . . acto

addict . . . . adicto

adjunct. . . . . adjunto

affect . . . . afecto

aqueduct . . . . acueducto

architect . . . . arquitecto

artifact . . . . artefacto

aspect . . . . **aspecto**

circumspect. . . . . circunspecto

compact . . . . compacto

conflict . . . . conflicto

contact . . . . **contacto**

contract . . . . **contrato**

    "The new contract is better." . . . **"El contrato nuevo es mejor"**.

convict . . . . convicto

correct . . . . **correcto**

defect	defecto
defunct	difunto
derelict	derelicto
dialect	**dialecto**
direct	**directo**

    "It's a direct flight." . . . . **"Es un vuelo directo".**

distinct	distinto *(meaning "different")*
district	distrito
edict	edicto
effect	efecto
exact	exacto
extinct	extinto
extract	extracto
impact	impacto
imperfect	imperfecto
incorrect	**incorrecto**

    "The answer is incorrect." . . . **"La respuesta es incorrecta".**

indirect	**indirecto**
indistinct	indistinto
inexact	inexacto
insect	insecto
instinct	instinto
intact	intacto
intellect	intelecto
object	objeto
pact	pacto
perfect	perfecto
prefect	prefecto
product	producto
project	proyecto
prospect	prospecto

select	. . . .	selecto *(only an adjective)*
strict	. . . .	estricto
succinct	. . . .	sucinto
tact	. . . .	tacto
verdict	. . . .	veredicto
viaduct	. . . .	viaducto

-ct/-cto

7A.

Una las palabras que están relacionadas o que son sinónimos.

1. correcto	ideal
2. perfecto	bien
3. incorrecto	parte
4. dialecto	mosca
5. acto	idioma
6. aspecto	mal
7. insecto	teatro

7B.

Escuche y lea el cuento. Responda las siguientes preguntas, usando oraciones completas.

Después de bajar del tren <u>directo</u> de Barcelona a Valencia, Angélica pregunta si éste es el lugar <u>correcto</u> porque ella no comprende nada. Ella sabe que el español hablado (spoken Spanish) no es siempre <u>perfecto</u>, ¡pero no comprende este acento ni un poquito! Juan dice, "No te preocupes (don't worry), tengo un buen <u>contacto</u> aquí en Valencia; se llama Alfonso, y él nos ayudará a conseguir los boletos". Después de unos minutos en la estación, Alfonso viene a recogerlos (pick them up). "Tiene <u>aspecto</u> de ser muy buena persona", dice Angélica. Alfonso es muy gracioso y tiene mucho respeto por su amigo Juan y su novia Angélica. Después de una buena cena en casa de Alfonso—la salsa estuvo <u>perfecta</u>—Angélica le pregunta si sabe algo sobre el baile en el centro. Alfonso responde, "Veremos...".

INSTANT Spanish Vocabulary Builder

1. ¿Qué tipo de tren tomaron de Barcelona?

2. ¿Por qué piensa Angélica que no es el lugar correcto?

3. ¿Por qué no comprende Angélica el español en Valencia?

4. ¿Cómo se llama el contacto de Juan en Valencia?

5. ¿Cómo estuvo la salsa de Alfonso?

English words ending in "–ence" often correspond to "–encia" in Spanish.

Spanish words ending in "–encia" are usually feminine nouns. For example,

a difference = *una diferencia*

ENGLISH. . . . . . . SPANISH	*All words and phrases in* **bold** *are on* **Track 8** *of the accompanying audio.*

absence . . . . **ausencia**
abstinence . . . . abstinencia
adherence . . . . adherencia
adolescence . . . . adolescencia
ambivalence . . . . ambivalencia
antiviolence . . . . antiviolencia
audience . . . . audiencia *(more commonly "público")*

belligerence . . . . beligerancia
beneficence . . . . beneficencia
benevolence . . . . benevolencia

cadence . . . . cadencia
circumference . . . . circunferencia
coexistence . . . . coexistencia
coherence . . . . coherencia
coincidence . . . . **coincidencia**
    "What a coincidence!" . . . . . **"¡Qué coincidencia!"**
competence . . . . competencia *(also used for "competition")*
complacence . . . . complacencia
condescendence . . . . condescendencia

condolence . . . . condolencia
conference . . . . **conferencia**
confidence . . . . confidencia *(meaning "secret/private information")*

confluence . . . . confluencia
congruence. . . . . congruencia
conscience . . . . conciencia
consequence . . . . **consecuencia**
consistence . . . . consistencia
continence . . . . continencia
convalescence. . . . . convalecencia
convenience . . . . conveniencia
convergence . . . . convergencia
corpulence . . . . corpulencia
correspondence. . . . . correspondencia

decadence . . . . decadencia
deference . . . . deferencia
dependence . . . . dependencia
difference . . . . **diferencia**
    "The difference is notable." . . . **"La diferencia es notable".**
diligence . . . . diligencia
disobedience . . . . desobediencia
dissidence . . . . disidencia
divergence . . . . divergencia

effervescence . . . . efervescencia
eloquence. . . . . elocuencia
emergence . . . . emergencia *(meaning "emergency")*
eminence . . . . eminencia
equivalence . . . . equivalencia
essence . . . . esencia
evidence . . . . evidencia
excellence . . . . excelencia
existence . . . . existencia
experience . . . . **experiencia**

fluorescence . . . . fluorescencia
frequence . . . . frecuencia *(also used for "frequency")*

imminence . . . . inminencia
impatience . . . . **impaciencia**
impermanence . . . . impermanencia
impertinence . . . . impertinencia
impotence . . . . impotencia
imprudence . . . . imprudencia
impudence . . . . impudencia
incandescence . . . . incandescencia
incidence . . . . incidencia *(also used for "impact," "effect")*
incoherence . . . . incoherencia
incompetence . . . . incompetencia
incongruence . . . . incongruencia
inconsequence . . . . inconsecuencia
inconsistence . . . . inconsistencia
incontinence . . . . incontinencia
inconvenience . . . . inconveniencia
independence . . . . independencia
indifference . . . . **indiferencia**
    "I hate indifference." . . . . **"Odio la indiferencia".**
indigence . . . . indigencia
indolence . . . . indolencia
indulgence . . . . indulgencia
inexistence . . . . inexistencia
inexperience . . . . inexperiencia
inference . . . . inferencia
influence . . . . **influencia**
infrequence . . . . infrecuencia
innocence . . . . **inocencia**
insistence . . . . insistencia
insolence . . . . insolencia
intelligence . . . . **inteligencia**

interdependence . . . . interdependencia
interference. . . . . interferencia
intransigence . . . . intransigencia
irreverence . . . . irreverencia

jurisprudence . . . . jurisprudencia

license . . . . licencia *(also used for "permit")*
luminescence . . . . luminiscencia

magnificence . . . . magnificencia
malevolence . . . . malevolencia
munificence . . . . munificencia

negligence . . . . negligencia
neuroscience. . . . . neurociencia

obedience . . . . obediencia
obsolescence . . . . obsolescencia
occurrence . . . . ocurrencia *(also used for*
                                        "bright idea")
omnipotence. . . . . omnipotencia
omnipresence . . . . omnipresencia
opulence . . . . opulencia

patience . . . . **paciencia**
  "Pedro has little patience.". . . . **"Pedro tiene poca paciencia".**
penitence . . . . penitencia
permanence . . . . permanencia
persistence . . . . persistencia
pertinence . . . . pertinencia
pestilence . . . . pestilencia
precedence. . . . . precedencia
preeminence. . . . . preeminencia
preexistence . . . . preexistencia
preference . . . . **preferencia**

presence. . . . . **presencia**
prominence. . . . . prominencia
providence . . . . providencia
prudence . . . . prudencia

quintessence . . . . quintaesencia

reference . . . . referencia
reminiscence. . . . . reminiscencia
residence . . . . **residencia**
reticence . . . . reticencia
reverence . . . . reverencia

science. . . . . **ciencia**
sentence. . . . . sentencia *(meaning "ruling")*
sequence . . . . **secuencia**
somnolence. . . . . somnolencia
subsistence . . . . subsistencia
succulence . . . . suculencia

teleconference. . . . . teleconferencia
transcendence. . . . . transcendencia
transference . . . . transferencia
transparence. . . . . trasparencia
truculence. . . . . truculencia
turbulence. . . . . turbulencia

vehemence . . . . vehemencia
videoconference . . . . videoconferencia
violence . . . . **violencia**
virulence. . . . . virulencia

8A.

Una las palabras que están relacionadas o que son sinónimos.

1. paciencia   prueba
2. conferencia   reunión
3. residencia   guerra
4. diferencia   liberación
5. violencia   casa
6. evidencia   esperar
7. independencia   distincion

8B.

Escuche y lea el cuento. Responda las siguientes preguntas, usando oraciones completas.

El día después, Alfonso le dice a Angélica, "¡Qué <u>coincidencia</u>! Mi novia y yo vamos al baile mañana por la noche, ¿queréis venir (do you two want to come) con nosotros?" El día después Angélica está muy contenta y le dice a Juan: "¿Ves? La <u>persistencia</u> y <u>diligencia</u> ayudan". Juan está muy contento por la felicidad de Angélica y piensa que será una buena <u>experiencia</u>. Desafortunadamente (unfortunately) Juan no tiene ni mucha <u>paciencia</u> ni mucho interés por el baile. Trata de esconder (he tries to hide) su <u>indiferencia</u>. Juan le dice a Angélica, "Lo siento por mi <u>impaciencia</u>, pero... ¡el baile está terrible!" Después de dos días con Alfonso en Valencia, Juan y Angélica van a Ibiza.

1. ¿Qué dice Alfonso del baile?

2. Según Angélica, ¿qué cosas ayudan?

3. ¿Qué expectativas (expectations) tiene Juan hacia el baile?

4. ¿A Juan le causa pasión o indiferencia el baile?

5. ¿Por qué pide disculpas (apologizes) Juan?

Chapter 9

English words ending in "–ent" often correspond to "–ente" in Spanish (excluding words ending in "–ment," which is a separate pattern).

Spanish words ending in "–ente" are usually adjectives or nouns. For example,

> innocent (adj.) = *inocente*
> client (n.) = *un/una cliente*

ENGLISH . . . . SPANISH

All words and phrases in **bold** *are on* **Track 9** *of the accompanying audio.*

absent . . . . ausente
absorbent . . . . absorbente
accident . . . . accidente
adherent . . . . adherente
adjacent . . . . adyacente
adolescent . . . . adolescente
agent . . . . **agente**
ambient . . . . ambiente *(meaning "environment")*
ambivalent . . . . ambivalente
antecedent . . . . antecedente
apparent . . . . aparente
ardent . . . . ardiente
astringent . . . . astringente

benevolent . . . . benevolente

client . . . . **cliente**
   "Miguel has no clients." . . . . . **"Miguel no tiene clientes".**
coefficient . . . . coeficiente

coexistent . . . . coexistente
coherent . . . . coherente
competent . . . . **competente**
complacent . . . . complaciente *(meaning "willing*
to please")

component . . . . componente
concupiscent . . . . concupiscente
concurrent . . . . concurrente
confident . . . . confidente *(meaning "a confidant")*
congruent . . . . congruente
consequent . . . . consiguiente
consistent . . . . consistente *(meaning "firm," "solid")*
constituent . . . . constituyente
continent . . . . **continente**
contingent . . . . contingente
convalescent . . . . convalesciente
convenient . . . . conveniente
convergent . . . . convergente
copresident . . . . copresidente
correspondent . . . . correspondiente
crescent . . . . creciente
current . . . . corriente

decadent . . . . decadente
decent . . . . decente
deficient . . . . deficiente
delinquent . . . . delincuente
dependent . . . . dependiente *(also used for "employee")*
descendent . . . . descendiente
detergent . . . . detergente
different . . . . **diferente**
    "I want something different." . . . . **"Quiero algo diferente".**
diligent . . . . diligente
disobedient . . . . desobediente
dissident . . . . disidente
dissolvent . . . . disolvente

divergent . . . . divergente

effervescent . . . . efervescente
efficient . . . . eficiente
eloquent. . . . . elocuente
emergent . . . . emergente
eminent . . . . eminente
equivalent. . . . . equivalente
evanescent . . . . evanescente
evident. . . . . evidente
excellent. . . . . excelente
exigent. . . . . exigente
existent. . . . . existente
exponent . . . . exponente

fervent . . . . ferviente
fluorescent . . . . fluorescente
frequent . . . . **frecuente**

imminent . . . . inminente
impatient . . . . **impaciente**
    "Carlos is very impatient." . . . **"Carlos es muy impaciente".**
impertinent . . . . impertinente
impotent. . . . . impotente
imprudent. . . . . imprudente
impudent . . . . impudente
incandescent. . . . . incandescente
incident . . . . incidente
incipient. . . . . incipiente
incoherent . . . . incoherente
incompetent . . . . incompetente
incongruent. . . . . incongruente
inconsistent. . . . . inconsistente *(meaning "flimsy")*
incontinent . . . . incontinente
inconvenient . . . . inconveniente *(also used for*
                                    "inconvenience")

indecent	indecente
independent	independiente
indifferent	**indiferente**
indigent	indigente
indolent	indolente
indulgent	indulgente
inefficient	ineficiente
inexistent	inexistente
infrequent	infrecuente
ingredient	**ingrediente**
inherent	inherente
innocent	**inocente**
insistent	insistente
insolent	insolente
insolvent	insolvente
insufficient	insuficiente
insurgent	insurgente
intelligent	**inteligente**

"Pablo is very intelligent." . . . **"Pablo es muy inteligente"**.

interdependent	interdependiente
intermittent	intermitente
intransigent	intransigente
iridescent	iridiscente
irreverent	irreverente
latent	latente
luminescent	luminiscente
magnificent	magnificente *(more commonly* "magnífico"*)*
munificent	munificente
nascent	naciente
negligent	negligente
nutrient	nutriente

INSTANT Spanish Vocabulary Builder

obedient. . . . . obediente
occident . . . . occidente
omnipotent . . . . omnipotente
omnipresent . . . . omnipresente
omniscient . . . . omnisciente
orient. . . . . oriente

parent . . . . pariente *(meaning "a relative")*
patent . . . . patente
patient. . . . . **paciente**
penitent . . . . penitente
permanent . . . . **permanente**
persistent . . . . persistente
pertinent. . . . . pertinente
pestilent . . . . pestilente
phosphorescent. . . . . fosforescente
potent . . . . potente
precedent. . . . . precedente
preeminent . . . . preeminente
preexistent . . . . preexistente
present. . . . . **presente**
president . . . . **presidente**
   "There's a new president." . . . **"Hay un presidente nuevo".**
prominent. . . . . prominente

quotient . . . . cociente

recent. . . . . reciente
recipient. . . . . recipiente *(also used for "container,"*
                                          "bowl")
recurrent. . . . . recurrente
redolent . . . . redolente
repellent. . . . . repelente
resident . . . . **residente**
reticent. . . . . reticente
reverent . . . . reverente

serpent . . . . serpiente
silent . . . . silente *(more commonly "silencioso")*
solvent . . . . solvente
strident . . . . estridente
subsequent . . . . subsiguiente
sufficient . . . . suficiente
superintendent . . . . superintendente

tangent . . . . **tangente**
torrent . . . . torrente
transcendent . . . . trascendente
transparent . . . . transparente
trident . . . . tridente

urgent . . . . **urgente**

vehement . . . . vehemente
vice president . . . . vicepresidente

9A.

Una las palabras que están relacionadas o que son sinónimos.

1. permanente   obvio
2. reciente   jefe
3. diferente   actual
4. presidente   nuevo
5. evidente   habitante
6. residente   fijo
7. presente   distinto

9B.

Escuche y lea el cuento. Responda las siguientes preguntas, usando oraciones completas.

Cuando llegan a Ibiza, Angélica llama a su madre y recibe un mensaje <u>urgente</u>: debe visitar a su primo (her cousin) **en Ibiza. Su primo Diego es el <u>presidente</u> de una compañía médica. Juan le dice, "Describe a tu primo, ¿cómo es?" Angélica responde, "Bueno, mi primo es... <u>diferente</u>... es un médico muy <u>competente</u> y muy, muy <u>inteligente</u>, pero es un poco extraño** (a bit strange)**". Juan quiere saber por qué es tan "<u>diferente</u>". Angélica le dice, "Ya verás** (you'll see)**, él piensa que todos somos médicos <u>residentes</u>". Juan dice, "Está bien, veremos...".**

1. ¿Qué tipo de mensaje recibe Angélica?

2. ¿Diego es el presidente de qué?

3. ¿Qué dice Angélica de su primo?

4. Según Angélica, ¿es Diego inteligente?

5. ¿Qué dice Juan al final?

-gy/-gía

Many English words ending in "–gy" correspond to "–gía" in Spanish.

Spanish words ending in "–gía" are usually feminine nouns. For example,

the energy = *la energía*

ENGLISH. . . . . . . SPANISH

All words and phrases in **bold** *are on* **Track 10** *of the accompanying audio.*

allergy . . . . **alergia**
    "Ana has a few allergies." . . . **"Ana tiene unas alergias"**.
analogy . . . . analogía
anesthesiology . . . . anestesiología
anthology . . . . antología
anthropology . . . . antropología
archaeology . . . . arqueología
astrology . . . . astrología
audiology . . . . audiología

biology . . . . **biología**
biotechnology . . . . biotecnología

cardiology . . . . cardiología
chronology . . . . **cronología**
climatology . . . . climatología
cosmetology . . . . cosmetología
cosmology . . . . cosmología
criminology . . . . criminología
cryptology . . . . criptología

dermatology . . . . dermatología

ecology . . . . ecología
Egyptology . . . . egiptología
elegy . . . . elegía
endocrinology . . . . endocrinología
energy . . . . **energía**
   "We need energy." . . . . **"Necesitamos energía".**
epidemiology . . . . epidemiología
ethnology . . . . etnología
etymology. . . . . etimología

gastroenterology . . . . gastroenterología
genealogy . . . . genealogía
geology . . . . **geología**
gynecology. . . . . ginecología

hydrology. . . . . hidrología

ideology. . . . . **ideología**

liturgy . . . . liturgia

meteorology . . . . **meteorología**
methodology. . . . . metodología
microbiology. . . . . microbiología
mineralogy . . . . mineralogía
morphology . . . . morfología
musicology . . . . musicología
mythology . . . . **mitología**

neurobiology . . . . neurobiología
neurology. . . . . neurología
numerology . . . . numerología

oncology . . . . oncología
ontology. . . . . ontología
ophthalmology . . . . oftalmología

orgy. . . . . orgía

paleontology. . . . . paleontología
parapsychology . . . . parasicología
pathology. . . . . patología
pedagogy. . . . . pedagogía
pharmacology. . . . . farmacología
philology . . . . filología
phonology . . . . fonología
phraseology . . . . fraseología
physiology . . . . fisiología
proctology . . . . proctología
psychology . . . . **psicología**
    "She studies psychology." . . . **"Ella estudia psicología"**.

radiology . . . . **radiología**
rheumatology . . . . reumatología

seismology . . . . sismología
sociology . . . . sociología
strategy . . . . **estrategia**
    "They have a strategy." . . . . . **"Ellos tienen una estrategia"**.
synergy . . . . sinergia

technology . . . . **tecnología**
terminology. . . . . terminología
theology. . . . . teología
topology. . . . . topología
toxicology. . . . . toxicología
trilogy . . . . **trilogía**
typology. . . . . tipología

urology . . . . urología

zoology . . . . zoología

10A.

Una las palabras que están relacionadas o que son sinónimos.

1. biología	historia
2. radiología	vida
3. tecnología	tres
4. trilogía	plan
5. estrategia	computadora
6. cronología	rayos X
7. geología	tierra

10B.

Escuche y lea el cuento. Responda las siguientes preguntas, usando oraciones completas.

A las nueve de la mañana Juan y Angélica van a la casa de Diego. El vive en San Miguel y es un hombre muy simpático y tiene mucha energía. Dice de pronto (suddenly), **"Hola muchachos, ¿tienen alguna alergia al café?" Los muchachos dicen que no y todos toman un café juntos. Diego empieza en seguida** (right away) **a hablar de nuevas tecnologías médicas y le pregunta a Juan si estudia radiología. Juan dice que nunca ha estudiado** (he never studied) **radiología pero sí hizo un año de biología. Diego le pregunta a Angélica si estudia psicología. Cuando ella dice que no, Diego dice, "Entonces, ¿estudias meteorología?" Angélica mira a Juan; él entiende rapidamente lo que significa "diferente".**

1. ¿Diego es perezoso (lazy) o tiene mucha energía?

2. ¿Los muchachos tienen alergia al café?

3. ¿De qué habla Diego?

4. ¿Estudia Juan radiología?

5. ¿Estudia Angélica psicología?

-ic/-ico

English words ending in "–ic" often correspond to "–ico" in Spanish.

Spanish words ending in "–ico" are usually adjectives. For example,

a <u>drastic</u> situation = *una situación <u>drastica</u>*

ENGLISH. . . . . . . SPANISH

All words and phrases in **bold** are on **Track 11** of the accompanying audio.

academic	académico
acoustic	acústico
acrobatic	acrobático
acrylic	acrílico
Adriatic	Adriático
aerobic	aeróbico
aerodynamic	aerodinámico
aeronautic	aeronáutico
aesthetic	estético
agnostic	agnóstico
alcoholic	**alcohólico**
"It's an alcoholic drink."	**"Es un trago alcohólico"**.
algebraic	algebraico
allergic	**alérgico**
alphabetic	alfabético
altruistic	altruístico *(more commonly "altruista")*
anabolic	anabólico
analytic	analítico
anarchic	anárquico
anatomic	anatómico
anemic	anémico

anesthetic . . . . anestésico

angelic. . . . . angélico *(more commonly "angelical")*

anorexic. . . . . anoréxico

antagonistic . . . . antagónico

antarctic. . . . . antártico

antibiotic . . . . antibiótico

anticlimactic . . . . anticlimático

antidemocratic . . . . antidemocrático

anti-Semitic . . . . antisemítico

antiseptic . . . . antiséptico

apologetic . . . . apologético

aquatic. . . . . acuático

Arabic . . . . arábico *(more commonly árabe)*

arctic . . . . ártico

archaic. . . . . arcaico

aristocratic . . . . aristocrático

arithmetic . . . . aritmético *(only an adjective)*

aromatic. . . . . aromático

artistic . . . . **artístico**

arthritic . . . . artrítico

asthmatic . . . . asmático

astronomic . . . . astronómico

asymmetric . . . . asimétrico

atheistic . . . . ateístico

athletic . . . . **atlético**

Atlantic . . . . Atlántico

atmospheric . . . . atmosférico

atomic . . . . atómico

attic . . . . ático

authentic . . . . **auténtico**

　　"The food is authentic." . . . . . **"La comida es auténtica".**

autistic . . . . autístico

autobiographic . . . . autobiográfico

autocratic . . . . autocrático

automatic . . . . automático

ballistic . . . . balístico

balsamic	balsámico
Baltic	báltico
barbaric	barbárico *(more commonly "bárbaro")*
barometric	barométrico
basic	básico
biographic	biográfico
bombastic	bombástico
botanic	botánico
bubonic	bubónico
bucolic	bucólico
bureaucratic	burocrático
calisthenic	calisténico
catastrophic	catastrófico
catatonic	catatónico
cathartic	catártico
Catholic	**católico**
caustic	cáustico
Celtic	céltico
ceramic	cerámico *(only an adjective, noun is "cerámica")*
chaotic	caótico
characteristic	característico
charismatic	carismático
choleric	colérico
chronic	**crónico**
chronologic	cronológico
citric	cítrico
civic	cívico
classic	**clásico**
"It's a classic book."	**"Es un libro clásico".**
climatic	climático
colic	cólico
comic	cómico *(also used for "comedian")*
concentric	concéntrico
cosmetic	cosmético

cosmic . . . . cósmico
critic . . . . crítico *(also used for "critical")*
cryptic . . . . críptico
cubic . . . . cúbico
cylindric . . . . cilíndrico
cynic . . . . cínico

democratic . . . . **democrático**
demographic . . . . demográfico
despotic . . . . despótico
diabetic . . . . diabético
diabolic . . . . diabólico
diagnostic . . . . diagnóstico
didactic . . . . didáctico
dietetic . . . . dietético
diplomatic . . . . diplomático
diuretic . . . . diurético
dogmatic . . . . dogmático
domestic . . . . **doméstico** *(for politics and flights,*
use "nacional")
doric . . . . dórico
dramatic . . . . dramático
drastic . . . . **drástico**
"The situation is not drastic.". . . . **"La situación no es drástica".**
dynamic . . . . dinámico
dyslexic . . . . disléxico

eccentric . . . . excéntrico
ecclesiastic . . . . eclesiástico
eclectic . . . . ecléctico
economic . . . . económico *(also used for "inexpensive")*
ecstatic . . . . extático
egocentric . . . . egocéntrico
elastic . . . . elástico
electric . . . . eléctrico
electromagnetic . . . . electromagnético

electronic . . . . **electrónico**
emblematic . . . . emblemático
emphatic . . . . enfático
energetic . . . . enérgico
enigmatic . . . . enigmático
enthusiastic . . . . entusiástico
epic . . . . épico
epileptic . . . . epiléptico
erotic . . . . erótico
erratic . . . . errático
esoteric . . . . esotérico
ethic . . . . ético
ethnic . . . . étnico
ethnocentric . . . . etnocéntrico
euphoric . . . . eufórico
evangelic . . . . evangélico
exotic . . . . **exótico**

fanatic . . . . fanático
fantastic . . . . **fantástico**
folic . . . . fólico
folkloric . . . . folclórico
forensic . . . . forénsico
frenetic . . . . frenético

galactic . . . . galáctico
gastric . . . . gástrico
gastronomic . . . . gastrónomico
generic . . . . genérico
genetic . . . . genético
geographic . . . . geográfico
geologic . . . . geológico
geometric . . . . geométrico
geriatric . . . . geriátrico
Germanic . . . . germánico
gothic . . . . gótico

graphic . . . . gráfico
gymnastic . . . . gimnástico

harmonic . . . . armónico
hedonistic . . . . hedonístico
hegemonic . . . . hegemónico
hemispheric . . . . hemisférico
heretic . . . . herético
heroic . . . . **heroico**
 "It was a heroic action." . . . . **"Fue una acción heroica"**.
hieroglyphic . . . . jeroglífico
Hispanic . . . . hispánico *(more commonly "hispano")*
historic . . . . **histórico**
histrionic . . . . histriónico
holistic . . . . holístico
homeopathic . . . . homeopático
Homeric . . . . homérico
hydraulic . . . . hidráulico
hygienic . . . . higiénico
hyperbolic . . . . hiperbólico
hypnotic . . . . hipnótico
hypodermic . . . . hipodérmico
hysteric . . . . histérico

ideologic . . . . ideológico
idiomatic . . . . idiomático
idyllic . . . . idílico
illogic . . . . ilógico
intrinsic . . . . intrínseco
ionic . . . . iónico
ironic . . . . **irónico**
 "It's an ironic situation." . . . . . **"Es una situación irónica"**.
Islamic . . . . islámico
isometric . . . . isométrico
italic . . . . itálico

INSTANT Spanish Vocabulary Builder

Jurassic . . . . Jurásico

kinetic . . . . cinético

laconic. . . . . lacónico
lethargic. . . . . letárgico
linguistic. . . . . lingüístico
lithographic . . . . litográfico
logic . . . . lógico (only an adjective;
           noun is "lógica")
logistic . . . . logístico
lunatic . . . . lunático
lyric . . . . lírico

macroeconomic. . . . . macroeconómico
magic . . . . mágico (only an adjective;
           noun is "magia")
magnetic . . . . magnético
mathematic. . . . . matemático
mechanic . . . . mecánico (also used for "mechanical")
medic. . . . . médico (also used for "medical")
melodic . . . . melódico
melodramatic . . . . melodramático
metabolic . . . . metabólico
metallic . . . . metálico
metalinguistic . . . . metalingüístico
metaphoric . . . . metafórico
metaphysic . . . . metafísico
meteoric. . . . . meteórico
methodic . . . . metódico
metric. . . . . **métrico**
microeconomic . . . . microeconómico
microscopic. . . . . **microscópico**
misanthropic. . . . . misantrópico
mnemonic. . . . . mnémonico
monopolistic . . . . monopolístico

mosaic . . . . mosaico

multiethnic . . . . multiétnico

mystic . . . . místico

mythic . . . . mítico

napoleonic . . . . napoleónico

narcotic . . . . narcótico

neurologic . . . . neurológico

neurotic . . . . neurótico

Nordic . . . . nórdico

nostalgic . . . . **nostálgico**

numeric . . . . numérico

oceanic . . . . oceánico

olympic . . . . olímpico *(for the sporting event,
use "olimpiadas")*

onomatopoeic . . . . onomatopéyico

optic . . . . óptico

organic . . . . orgánico

orgasmic . . . . orgásmico

orthopedic . . . . ortopédico

Pacific . . . . Pacífico

panic . . . . **pánico**

Paleozoic . . . . Paleozoico

panoramic . . . . panorámico

parasitic . . . . parasítico

pathetic . . . . **patético**

pathologic . . . . patológico

patriotic . . . . **patriótico**

   "The people are very patriotic." . . . **"El público es muy patriótico".**

pediatric . . . . pediátrico

periodic . . . . periódico *(also used
for "newspaper")*

phallic . . . . fálico

philanthropic . . . . filantrópico

philosophic............	filosófico
phobic...............	fóbico
phonetic..............	fonético
photogenic............	fotogénico
photographic	fotográfico
plastic	plástico
platonic	platónico
pneumatic.............	pneumático *(also used for "tire")*
poetic...............	**poético**
polemic	polémico
pornographic	pornográfico
pragmatic.............	pragmático
prehistoric	prehistórico
problematic	problemático
prolific	prolífico
prophetic	profético
prophylactic	profiláctico
prosaic...............	prosaico
prosthetic	protésico
psychedelic............	psicodélico
psychiatric	psiquiátrico
psychic...............	psíquico
psychopathic...........	psicopático
psychotic	psicótico
pubic................	púbico
public	público *(also used for "audience")*
rhetoric	retórico
rheumatic.............	reumático
rhythmic..............	rítmico
robotic...............	robótico
romantic..............	**romántico**
"It's a romantic city."	**"Es una ciudad romántica".**
rustic	rústico
sadistic...............	sádico

sarcastic	**sarcástico**
sardonic	sardónico
satanic	satánico
satiric	satírico
scenic	escénico
schematic	esquemático
schizophrenic	esquizofrénico
scholastic	escolástico
scientific	**científico**
semantic	semántico
semiautomatic	semiautomático
semiotic	semiótico
septic	séptico
skeptic	escéptico
sociolinguistic	sociolingüístico
sonic	sónico
soporific	soporífico
spasmodic	espasmódico
spastic	espástico
specific	**específico**
spheric	esférico
sporadic	esporádico
static	estático
statistic	estadístico
stoic	estoico
strategic	**estratégico**
stylistic	estilístico
subatomic	subatómico
supersonic	supersónico
symbolic	**simbólico**
"It's a symbolic gift."	**"Es un regalo simbólico".**
symmetric	simétrico
symptomatic	sintomático
synthetic	sintético
systematic	sistemático

telegenic	telegénico
telegraphic	telegráfico
telepathic	telepático
telescopic	telescópico
terrific	terrífico *(meaning "terrifying")*
thematic	temático
theoretic	teórico
therapeutic	terapeutico
titanic	titánico
tonic	tónico
topic	tópico
touristic	turístico
toxic	tóxico
traffic	tráfico
tragic	trágico
traumatic	traumático
tropic	trópico
ultrasonic	ultrasónico
volcanic	volcánico

11A.

Una las palabras que están relacionadas o que son sinónimos.

1. pragmático	práctico
2. trafico	detalles
3. auténtico	amoroso
4. específico	carros
5. electrónico	intemporal
6. clásico	estéreo
7. romántico	verdadero

11B.

Escuche y lea el cuento. Responda las siguientes preguntas, usando oraciones completas.

Después de dos días en Ibiza, Juan y Angélica van a Alicante. Alicante es bellísima, de una belleza <u>clásica</u>. Durante el día (during the day) **van a algunos museos <u>artísticos</u>, y por la noche ven lo <u>mágico</u> que es Alicante. No hay una explicación <u>específica</u>, pero Alicante es una ciudad <u>fantástica</u>. Juan conduce un carro alquilado** (rented car), **pero hay mucho <u>tráfico</u>. Angélica dice que no es un plan muy <u>estratégico</u>. En Alicante hay siempre mucho <u>tráfico</u> en el verano. Ella dice, "El tren es mejor** (better), **no es muy <u>romántico</u> pasar las vacaciones dentro de un carro". Juan responde, "Veremos...".**

1. ¿Cuál es el problema cuando Juan conduce?

2. ¿Por qué dice Angélica, "El tren es mejor"?

3. ¿Qué tipos de museos visitan?

4. ¿Cuándo es mágico Alicante?

5. ¿Qué tipo de ciudad es Alicante?

-ical/-ico

Many English words ending in "–ical" correspond to "–ico" in Spanish.

Spanish words ending in "–ico" are usually adjectives. For example,

<u>identical</u> twins = *gemelos* <u>*idénticos*</u>

ENGLISH....... SPANISH

All words and phrases in **bold** *are on* **Track 12** *of the accompanying audio.*

acoustical . . . . acústico
aeronautical . . . . aeronáutico
allegorical . . . . alegórico
alphabetical . . . . **alfabético**
    "It's in alphabetical order." . . . **"Está en orden alfabético"**.
analytical . . . . analítico
anarchical . . . . anárquico
anatomical . . . . anatómico
antithetical . . . . antitético
apolitical . . . . apolítico
archaeological . . . . **arqueológico**
astrological . . . . astrológico
astronomical . . . . astronómico
asymmetrical . . . . asimétrico
atypical . . . . atípico
autobiographical . . . . autobiográfico

biblical . . . . bíblico
bibliographical . . . . bibliográfico
biochemical . . . . bioquímico
biographical . . . . biográfico
biological . . . . **biológico**

botanical . . . . **botánico**

categorical . . . . categórico
chemical. . . . . químico
chronological . . . . cronológico
classical . . . . clásico
clinical . . . . clínico
comical . . . . cómico *(also used for "comedian")*
critical . . . . **crítico** *(also used for "critic")*
cubical. . . . . cúbico
cyclical. . . . . cíclico
cylindrical. . . . . cilíndrico
cynical . . . . **cínico**

demographical . . . . demográfico
diabolical. . . . . diabólico
dialectical. . . . . dialéctico

ecclesiastical. . . . . eclesiástico
ecological. . . . . ecológico
economical . . . . económico
electrical. . . . . **eléctrico**
elliptical . . . . elíptico
empirical . . . . empírico
ethical . . . . ético
evangelical. . . . . evangélico

fanatical. . . . . fanático

gastronomical . . . . gastronómico
genealogical. . . . . genealógico
geographical . . . . geográfico
geological . . . . geológico
geometrical. . . . . geométrico
grammatical . . . . gramático

hierarchical . . . . jerárquico
historical . . . . histórico
hypothetical . . . . hipotético
hysterical . . . . histérico

identical . . . . **idéntico**
    "They are identical twins." . . . **"Son gemelos idénticos"**.
ideological . . . . ideológico
illogical . . . . ilógico
impractical . . . . impráctico
ironical. . . . . irónico
lexical . . . . léxico *(meaning "lexicon,"*
                                "vocabulary")

logical . . . . **lógico**
logistical. . . . . logístico
lyrical. . . . . lírico

magical . . . . **mágico**
mathematical . . . . matemático
mechanical. . . . . mecánico *(also used for "mechanic")*
medical . . . . médico *(also used for "doctor,"*
                                 "medic")
metaphorical. . . . . metafórico
metaphysical. . . . . metafísico
methodical . . . . metódico
musical. . . . . músico
mystical . . . . místico
mythical . . . . mítico
mythological . . . . mitológico

nautical . . . . náutico
neurological . . . . neurológico
numerical . . . . numérico

optical . . . . óptico

paradoxical . . . . paradójico

pathological . . . . patológico

pedagogical . . . . pedagógico

periodical . . . . periódico *(also used for "newspaper")*

pharmaceutical . . . . farmaceutico *(also used for "pharmacist")*

philosophical . . . . filosófico

physical . . . . físico

physiological . . . . fisiológico

poetical . . . . poético

political . . . . político

practical . . . . **práctico**

    "She is very practical." . . . . . **"Ella es muy práctica"**.

prehistorical . . . . prehistórico

psychological . . . . psicológico

reciprocal . . . . recíproco

rhetorical . . . . retórico

rhythmical . . . . rítmico

sabbatical . . . . sabático

satirical . . . . satírico

skeptical . . . . escéptico

sociological . . . . sociológico

sociopolitical . . . . sociopolítico

spherical . . . . esférico

statistical . . . . estadístico

stereotypical . . . . estereotípico

stoical . . . . estoico

strategical . . . . estratégico

symmetrical . . . . simétrico

tactical . . . . táctico

technical . . . . **técnico** *(also used for "technician")*

technological . . . . tecnológico

theological . . . . teológico

theoretical . . . . teórico
topical . . . . tópico
typical . . . . **típico**
    "What a typical response!" . . . **"¡Qué respuesta típica!"**
typographical . . . . tipográfico
tyrannical . . . . tiránico

12A.

Una las palabras que están relacionadas o que son sinónimos.

1. típico	pragmático
2. idéntico	importante
3. práctico	usual
4. biográfico	personal
5. diabólico	médico
6. clínico	demoníaco
7. crítico	igual

12B.

Escuche y lea el cuento. Responda las siguientes preguntas, usando oraciones completas.

Juan dice, "Alicante es tan bonita que podemos pasar el mes entero (the whole month) **aquí**". Angélica comprende pero dice, "No, quiero ser <u>práctica</u>, debemos continuar nuestro viaje de una manera <u>lógica</u>". Juan ve que ella es muy <u>lógica</u> ahora y dice, "Angélica, ésto es <u>típico</u> de tí, ¡eres siempre tan <u>práctica</u>!" Ella responde, "¡No seas tan <u>crítico</u>! Tú también quieres ir a la Costa del Sol, ¿verdad?" Juan responde, "Tienes razón (you're right), vamos a la Costa del Sol".

1. ¿ Juan quiere permanecer (to stay) en Alicante o partir?

2. ¿De qué manera quiere viajar Angélica?

3. ¿Angélica es siempre práctica?

4. ¿Adónde van ahora?

5. ¿Qué dice Angélica de la Costa del Sol?

-ical/-ico

-id/-ido

Many English words ending in "–id" correspond to "–ido" in Spanish.

Spanish words ending in "–ido" are usually adjectives. For example,

a <u>splendid</u> plan = *un plan <u>espléndido</u>*

ENGLISH. . . . . . . SPANISH

All words and phrases in **bold** *are on* **Track 13** *of the accompanying audio.*

ENGLISH	SPANISH
acid	ácido
antacid	antiácido
arid	árido
avid	ávido
candid	cándido *(meaning "innocent," "naïve")*
Cupid	Cupido
fervid	férvido
flaccid	flácido
florid	florido
fluid	fluido
frigid	frígido
hybrid	híbrido
insipid	insípido
intrepid	intrépido
invalid	inválido
languid	lánguido

liquid . . . . **líquido**
livid . . . . lívido
lucid . . . . lúcido

morbid . . . . mórbido

pallid . . . . pálido
placid . . . . plácido
putrid . . . . pútrido

rapid . . . . **rápido**
rigid . . . . **rígido**

solid . . . . sólido
sordid . . . . sórdido
splendid . . . . **espléndido**
    "He has a splendid plan." . . . **"El tiene un plan espléndido"**.
squallid . . . . escuálido
stupid . . . . **estúpido**

timid . . . . **tímido**
    "Mateo is very timid." . . . . . . **"Mateo es muy tímido"**.
torrid . . . . tórrido

valid . . . . **válido**
vivid . . . . vívido

13A.

Una las palabras que están relacionadas o que son sinónimos.

1. rápido	maravilloso
2. tímido	limón
3. estúpido	veloz
4. ácido	introvertido
5. frígido	seco
6. árido	helado
7. espléndido	idiota

13B.

Escuche y lea el cuento. Responda las siguientes preguntas, usando oraciones completas.

Para ir a la Costa del Sol, Juan y Angélica deciden alquilar (to rent) **otro carro. Angélica dice que es un plan estúpido, pero Juan piensa que es un plan espléndido. Angélica dice, "Pero yo quiero viajar mas rápido…". Juan dice que prefiere conducir cuando hace calor. Durante el viaje hace un tiempo** (the weather is) **muy húmedo; de repente Juan se pone muy pálido y le duele el estómago. Angélica no dice nada y va a una farmacia y compra un poco de antiácido para Juan. El farmacéutico dice que él debe beber mucho líquido y no comer comida ácida.**

1. ¿Qué dice Angélica del plan de ir a la Costa del Sol en carro?

2. ¿Qué piensa Juan de su idea?

3. ¿Qué tiempo hace durante el viaje?

4. ¿Qué le compra Angélica a Juan cuando él se siente mal?

5. ¿El farmacéutico dice que debe beber qué? ¿Y qué no debe comer?

-ism/-ismo

English words ending in "–ism" often correspond to "–ismo" in Spanish.

Spanish words ending in "–ism" are usually masculine nouns. For example,

optimism = *el optimismo*

ENGLISH . . . . SPANISH

All words and phrases in **bold** *are on* **Track 14** *of the accompanying audio.*

absenteeism . . . . absentismo
absolutism . . . . absolutismo
activism . . . . activismo
adventurism . . . . aventurismo
alcoholism . . . . **alcoholismo**
altruism . . . . altruismo
Americanism. . . . . americanismo
amorphism . . . . amorfismo
anachronism. . . . . anacronismo
anarchism. . . . . anarquismo
Anglicism . . . . anglicismo
antagonism. . . . . antagonismo
anticapitalism . . . . anticapitalismo
anticommunism . . . . anticomunismo
antifascism . . . . **antifascismo**
    "There was a lot of antifascism.". . . **"Había mucho antifascismo"**.
anti-Semitism. . . . . antisemitismo
antiterrorism . . . . antiterrorismo
astigmatism. . . . . astigmatismo
atheism . . . . ateísmo
athleticism . . . . **atletismo** *(also used for "track-and-field")*
autism . . . . autismo

baptism . . . . bautismo
bipolarism . . . . bipolarismo
botulism . . . . botulismo
Buddhism . . . . budismo

cannibalism . . . . canibalismo
capitalism. . . . . **capitalismo**
    "Capitalism comes   **"El capitalismo viene**
    from America.". . . . . **de América".**
Catholicism. . . . . catolicismo
catechism . . . . catecismo
centralism. . . . . centralismo
chauvinism . . . . chovinismo
classicism . . . . clasicismo
colonialism . . . . colonialismo
communism . . . . **comunismo**
conformism. . . . . conformismo
conservatism. . . . . conservatismo
criticism . . . . criticismo *(more commonly "crítica")*
cubism . . . . cubismo
cynicism. . . . . cinismo

Darwinism . . . . darwinismo
deism. . . . . deísmo
despotism. . . . . despotismo
determinism . . . . determinismo
dogmatism . . . . dogmatismo
dualism . . . . dualismo

egoism. . . . . egoísmo *(meaning "selfishness")*
egotism . . . . egotismo
elitism . . . . elitismo
eroticism. . . . . erotismo
euphemism . . . . eufemismo
evangelism . . . . evangelismo
evolutionism . . . . evolucionismo

exorcism . . . . exorcismo
expressionism . . . . expresionismo
extremism . . . . extremismo

fanaticism . . . . fanatismo
fascism . . . . **fascismo**
    "I don't like fascism." . . . . **"No me gusta el fascismo".**
fatalism . . . . fatalismo
favoritism . . . . favoritismo
federalism . . . . federalismo
feminism . . . . **feminismo**
feudalism . . . . feudalismo
fundamentalism . . . . fundamentalismo
futurism . . . . futurismo

globalism . . . . globalismo

hedonism . . . . hedonismo
heroism . . . . heroísmo
Hinduism . . . . hinduismo
humanism . . . . humanismo
humanitarianism . . . . humanitarismo
hypnotism . . . . hipnotismo

idealism . . . . idealismo
imperialism . . . . imperialismo
impressionism . . . . **impresionismo**
individualism . . . . individualismo
Italianism . . . . italianismo

Judaism . . . . judaismo

Latinism . . . . latinismo
lesbianism . . . . lesbianismo
liberalism . . . . liberalismo
localism . . . . localismo

magnetism	magnetismo
Marxism	marxismo
materialism	materialismo
mechanism	**mecanismo**
metabolism	metabolismo
microorganism	microorganismo
minimalism	minimalismo
modernism	modernismo
monotheism	monoteísmo
multiculturalism	multiculturalismo

nationalism	**nacionalismo**

"There is a lot of nationalism." ... **"Hay mucho nacionalismo"**.

naturalism	naturalismo
Nazism	nazismo
negativism	negativismo
neofascism	neofascismo
neologism	neologismo
neo-Nazism	neonazismo
neorealism	neorrealismo
nepotism	nepotismo
nudism	nudismo

objectivism	objetivismo
occultism	ocultismo
opportunism	oportunismo
optimism	**optimismo**

"Optimism always helps." ... **"El optimismo ayuda siempre"**.

organism	**organismo**

paganism	paganismo
parallelism	paralelismo
passivism	pasivismo
patriotism	patriotismo
pessimism	pesimismo
pluralism	pluralismo

polytheism	politeísmo
populism	populismo
positivism	positivismo
postmodernism	posmodernismo
pragmatism	pragmatismo
primitivism	primitivismo
professionalism	**profesionalismo**
protectionism	proteccionismo
Protestantism	protestantismo
provincialism	provincialismo
purism	purismo
Puritanism	puritanismo

racism	**racismo**
radicalism	radicalismo
rationalism	racionalismo
realism	realismo
reformism	reformismo
regionalism	regionalismo
relativism	relativismo
romanticism	romanticismo

sadism	sadismo
satanism	satanismo
sensationalism	sensacionalismo
sensualism	sensualismo
separatism	separatismo
sexism	sexismo
socialism	**socialismo**
spiritualism	espiritualismo
Stalinism	estalinismo
stoicism	estoicismo
structuralism	estructuralismo
surrealism	surrealismo
syllogism	silogismo
symbolism	simbolismo

synchronism . . . . sincronismo

terrorism . . . . **terrorismo**
    "Terrorism is senseless." . . . . . **"El terrorismo no tiene sentido".**
totalitarianism . . . . totalitarismo
tourism. . . . . **turismo**
traditionalism . . . . tradicionalismo
transcendentalism . . . . trascendentalismo
traumatism . . . . traumatismo
truism. . . . . truismo

utilitarianism . . . . utilitarismo

vandalism. . . . . vandalismo
vegetarianism . . . . vegetarianismo
voyeurism. . . . . voyeurismo

14A.

Una las palabras que están relacionadas o que son sinónimos.

1. turismo	olímpico
2. comunismo	nación
3. patriotismo	Karl Marx
4. atletismo	comentario
5. terrorismo	positivo
6. optimismo	bomba
7. criticismo	vacaciones

14B.

Escuche y lea el cuento. Responda las siguientes preguntas, usando oraciones completas.

Después de su primer día en la Costa del Sol, Juan se siente mejor. Hay mucho <u>turismo</u> en la Costa del Sol, y mucha historia, pero ellos deciden relajarse (decide to relax) **por algunos días en la playa. Angélica compra un libro de historia española y lee sobre el comienzo** (about the beginning) **del <u>fascismo</u> en España durante los años treinta. También lee sobre la influencia del <u>comunismo</u> y del <u>socialismo</u> en España. Ellos hablan sobre el <u>patriotismo</u> español, y Angélica le pregunta a Juan qué piensa sobre** (what he thinks about) **el <u>capitalismo</u>. Juan dice, "Angélica, todo esto es muy interesante pero... ¡tomemos un helado!"**

1. ¿Hay mucho turismo en la Costa del Sol?

2. ¿Cuándo comenzó el fascismo en España?

3. ¿ Angélica lee sobre la influencia de qué en España?

4. ¿Sobre qué hablan?

5. ¿Qué dice Juan al final?

-ist/-ista

Many English words ending in "–ist" correspond to "–ista" in Spanish.

Spanish words ending in "–ista" are usually nouns. For example,

an artist = *un/una artista*

Chapter 15

ENGLISH . . . . SPANISH

All words and phrases in **bold** *are on* **Track 15** *of the accompanying audio.*

abolitionist . . . . abolicionista
activist . . . . activista
acupuncturist. . . . . acupuncturista
adventurist . . . . aventurista
alchemist . . . . alquemista
altruist . . . . altruista
analyst . . . . analista
anarchist . . . . anarquista
anatomist . . . . anatomista
antagonist . . . . antagonista
anticommunist. . . . . anticomunista
antifascist . . . . antifascista
artist . . . . **artista**
   "That artist is creative." . . . . . **"Ese artista es creativo".**
atheist . . . . ateísta *(more commonly "ateo")*

Baptist . . . . bautista
botanist . . . . botanista
Buddhist. . . . . budista

capitalist. . . . . **capitalista**
caricaturist . . . . caricaturista

cellist . . . . violoncelista
centralist . . . . centralista
chauvinist . . . . chovinista
columnist . . . . columnista
communist . . . . **comunista**
conformist . . . . conformista
conservationist . . . . conservacionista
contortionist . . . . contorsionista
cubist . . . . cubista
cyclist . . . . ciclista

dentist . . . . **dentista**
    "Her son is a dentist." . . . . . . **"Su hijo es un dentista".**
dualist . . . . dualista
duelist . . . . duelista

ecologist . . . . ecologista
economist . . . . economista
egoist . . . . egoísta
egotist . . . . egotista
elitist . . . . elitista
essayist . . . . ensayista
evangelist . . . . evangelista
exhibitionist . . . . exhibicionista
existentialist . . . . existencialista
expansionist . . . . expansionista
expressionist . . . . expresionista
extremist . . . . extremista

fascist . . . . fascista
fatalist . . . . fatalista
federalist . . . . federalista
feminist . . . . feminista
finalist . . . . **finalista**
flutist . . . . flautista
florist . . . . **florista**

formalist . . . . formalista
fundamentalist . . . . fundamentalista
futurist . . . . futurista

geneticist . . . . geneticista
guitarist . . . . **guitarrista**
   "Carlos Santana is   **"Carlos Santana es**
   a great guitarist." . . . . **un gran guitarrista".**

harpist . . . . arpista
hedonist . . . . hedonista
humanist . . . . humanista
humorist . . . . humorista
hygienist . . . . higienista

idealist . . . . **idealista**
illusionist . . . . ilusionista
imperialist . . . . imperialista
impressionist . . . . impresionista
individualist . . . . individualista
internist . . . . internista
isolationist . . . . aislacionista

jurist . . . . jurista

Latinist . . . . latinista
Leninist . . . . leninista
linguist . . . . lingüista
list . . . . **lista**
   "She has a list of questions." . . . **"Ella tiene una lista de preguntas".**

machinist . . . . maquinista
manicurist . . . . manicurista
Marxist . . . . marxista
masochist . . . . masoquista
materialist . . . . materialista

Methodist	metodista
minimalist	**minimalista**
modernist	modernista
monopolist	monopolista
moralist	moralista
motorist	motorista
muralist	muralista
narcissist	narcisista
nationalist	nacionalista
naturalist	naturalista
novelist	novelista
nudist	nudista
nutritionist	**nutricionista**
opportunist	oportunista
optimist	**optimista**
organist	organista
orthodontist	ortodontista
pacifist	pacifista
perfectionist	perfeccionista
pessimist	**pesimista**
pianist	**pianista**

"He wants to be a pianist." . . **"Quisiera ser pianista".**

pluralist	pluralista
populist	populista
positivist	positivista
pragmatist	pragmatista
prohibitionist	prohibicionista
protagonist	protagonista
protectionist	proteccionista
publicist	publicista
purist	purista
racist	**racista**

rationalist . . . . racionalista
realist. . . . . **realista**
receptionist . . . . recepcionista
reformist . . . . reformista
reservist . . . . reservista

sadomasochist . . . . sadomasoquista
satanist . . . . satanista
satirist . . . . satirista
secessionist . . . . secesionista
semifinalist . . . . semifinalista
separatist . . . . separatista
sexist . . . . sexista
socialist . . . . socialista
soloist . . . . solista
specialist . . . . especialista
Stalinist . . . . estalinista
stylist . . . . estilista
surrealist . . . . surrealista
symbolist . . . . simbolista

terrorist . . . . **terrorista**
tourist . . . . **turista**
    "In Spain, I'm a tourist." . . . . **"En España, soy turista"**.
traditionalist . . . . tradicionalista

violinist . . . . violinista
vocalist . . . . vocalista

15A.

Una las palabras que están relacionadas o que son sinónimos.

1. artista	dinero
2. dentista	pasaporte
3. turista	campeón
4. pesimista	cantante
5. idealista	positivo
6. finalista	diente
7. capitalista	negativo

15B.

Escuche y lea el cuento. Responda las siguientes preguntas, usando oraciones completas.

Destinación: ¡Andalucía! Mientras Juan y Angélica pasean por (walk around) **Andalucía conocen otra pareja** (another couple) **de Bilbao. El muchacho es <u>dentista</u> y la muchacha es <u>artista</u>; los nuevos amigos de Juan y Angélica son <u>turistas</u> "profesionales"; viajan mucho y saben mucho sobre Andalucía. Angélica tiene una <u>lista</u> de preguntas y el <u>dentista</u> puede dar una respuesta a cada** (every) **pregunta. Son muy inteligentes pero son una pareja extraña. La muchacha es <u>optimista</u> mientras que el muchacho es <u>pesimista</u>. Ella es <u>idealista</u> y él es <u>realista</u>. El <u>dentista</u> les dice a Juan y Angélica, "¿Queréis ir a Málaga con nosostros?" Juan responde, "Veremos...".**

INSTANT Spanish Vocabulary Builder

1. ¿Qué hace el muchacho que conocen?

-ist/-ista

2. ¿Los nuevos amigos de Juan y Angélica viajan a menudo (often)?

3. ¿De qué tiene una lista Angélica?

4. ¿Cómo es el dentista?

5. ¿Cómo es la artista?

-ive/-ivo

English words ending in "–ive" often correspond to "–ivo" in Spanish.

Spanish words ending in "–ivo" are usually adjectives. For example,

a <u>competitive</u> boy = *un niño <u>competitivo</u>*

All words and phrases in **bold** *are on* **Track 16** *of the accompanying audio.*

ENGLISH....... SPANISH

abortive . . . . abortivo
abrasive. . . . . abrasivo
abusive . . . . abusivo
accumulative. . . . . acumulativo
accusative . . . . acusativo
active. . . . . **activo**
    "It's not an active volcano." . . . **"No es un volcán activo".**
addictive . . . . adictivo
additive . . . . aditivo
adhesive. . . . . adhesivo
adjective. . . . . **adjetivo**
administrative . . . . administrativo
adoptive. . . . . adoptivo
affective . . . . afectivo
affirmative . . . . afirmativo
aggressive . . . . **agresivo**
allusive. . . . . alusivo
alternative . . . . alternativo
anticorrosive. . . . . anticorrosivo
appositive. . . . . apositivo
apprehensive . . . . aprensivo
archive. . . . . archivo

assertive . . . . asertivo

associative . . . . asociativo

attractive . . . . atractivo

attributive . . . . atributivo

augmentative . . . . aumentativo

authoritive . . . . autoritativo *(more commonly
"autoritario")*

captive . . . . cautivo

causative . . . . causativo

coactive . . . . coactivo

cognitive . . . . cognitivo

cohesive . . . . cohesivo

collaborative . . . . colaborativo

collective . . . . colectivo

combative . . . . combativo

commemorative . . . . conmemorativo

communicative . . . . comunicativo

comparative . . . . comparativo

competitive . . . . **competitivo**

   "The kids are   **"Los niños son**

      so competitive." . . . . **tan competitivos".**

comprehensive . . . . comprensivo *(meaning "understanding")*

compulsive . . . . compulsivo

conclusive . . . . conclusivo

conductive . . . . conductivo

conflictive . . . . conflictivo

connective . . . . conectivo

consecutive . . . . **consecutivo**

conservative . . . . conservativo *(more commonly
"conservador")*

constructive . . . . constructivo

contemplative . . . . contemplativo

contributive . . . . contributivo

convulsive . . . . convulsivo

cooperative . . . . **cooperativo**

INSTANT Spanish Vocabulary Builder

coordinative . . . . coordinativo
corrective . . . . correctivo
corrosive . . . . corrosivo
corruptive . . . . corruptivo
creative . . . . **creativo**
cumulative . . . . acumulativo
curative . . . . curativo
cursive . . . . cursivo

dative . . . . dativo
decisive . . . . decisivo
declarative . . . . declarativo
decorative . . . . decorativo
deductive . . . . deductivo
defensive . . . . defensivo *(only used to describe things)*
definitive . . . . **definitivo**
"It's a definitive plan." . . . . . . **"Es un plan definitivo".**
degenerative . . . . degenerativo
deliberative . . . . deliberativo
demonstrative . . . . demostrativo
denominative . . . . denominativo
depressive . . . . depresivo
derivative . . . . derivativo
descriptive . . . . descriptivo
destructive . . . . destructivo
determinative . . . . determinativo
diffusive . . . . difusivo
digestive . . . . digestivo
diminutive . . . . diminutivo
directive . . . . directivo
distinctive . . . . distintivo
distributive . . . . distributivo
divisive . . . . divisivo

educative . . . . educativo

effective . . . . efectivo *(also used for "cash")*

elective. . . . . electivo

elusive . . . . elusivo

emotive . . . . emotivo *(meaning "emotional")*

erosive. . . . . erosivo

evasive. . . . . evasivo

evocative . . . . evocativo

excessive . . . . **excesivo**

exclusive . . . . exclusivo

executive . . . . **ejecutivo**

exhaustive . . . . exhaustivo

expansive. . . . . expansivo

explicative . . . . explicativo

explorative . . . . explorativo *(more commonly "exploratorio")*

explosive . . . . explosivo

expressive . . . . expresivo

extensive . . . . extensivo

festive . . . . festivo *(also used for "of a holiday")*

figurative . . . . figurativo

formative . . . . formativo

fugitive. . . . . fugitivo

furtive. . . . . furtivo

generative . . . . generativo

hyperactive. . . . . hiperactivo

illuminative . . . . iluminativo

illustrative . . . . ilustrativo

imaginative. . . . . **imaginativo**

    "What an imaginative plan!". . . **"¡Qué plan tan imaginativo!"**

imitative. . . . . imitativo

imperative . . . . imperativo

implosive . . . . implosivo

impulsive . . . . impulsivo
inactive . . . . inactivo
incentive. . . . . incentivo
incisive. . . . . incisivo
inclusive . . . . inclusivo
indicative . . . . indicativo
infinitive . . . . infinitivo
informative . . . . informativo
inoffensive . . . . inofensivo
inquisitive. . . . . inquisitivo
instinctive . . . . instintivo
instructive . . . . instructivo
intensive. . . . . intensivo
interactive. . . . . **interactivo**
interpretative. . . . . interpretativo
interrogative . . . . interrogativo
intransitive . . . . intransitivo
introspective . . . . introspectivo
intuitive . . . . intuitivo
inventive. . . . . inventivo

legislative . . . . legislativo
lucrative . . . . lucrativo

massive . . . . masivo
motive . . . . motivo
multiplicative. . . . . multiplicativo

narrative. . . . . narrativo
native. . . . . nativo
negative . . . . **negativo**
  "Don't be so negative!" . . . . . **"¡No seas tan negativo!"**
nominative . . . . nominativo

objective. . . . . **objetivo**
obsessive . . . . obsesivo

offensive	**ofensivo**
olive	olivo *(meaning "olive tree")*
operative	operativo
oppressive	opresivo
partitive	partitivo
passive	pasivo
pejorative	peyorativo
pensive	pensativo
perceptive	perceptivo
permissive	permisivo
persuasive	persuasivo
positive	**positivo**
possessive	**posesivo**
preparative	preparativo
prescriptive	preceptivo
presumptive	presuntivo
preventive	preventivo
primitive	**primitivo**
productive	**productivo**
progressive	progresivo
prohibitive	prohibitivo
prospective	prospectivo
provocative	provocativo
punitive	punitivo
qualitative	cualitativo
quantitative	cuantitativo
radioactive	radiactivo
reactive	reactivo
receptive	receptivo
recessive	recesivo
recreative	recreativo
reflexive	reflexivo
regressive	regresivo

relative. . . . . relativo *(only an adjective)*

repetitive . . . . **repetitivo**

"It's a repetitive exercise." . . . **"Es un ejercicio repetitivo"**.

repulsive. . . . . repulsivo

representative . . . . representativo *(only an adjective)*

repressive. . . . . represivo

reproductive . . . . reproductivo

respective. . . . . respectivo

restorative. . . . . restaurativo

restrictive . . . . restrictivo

retentive . . . . retentivo

retroactive . . . . retroactivo

retrospective . . . . retrospectivo

sedative . . . . sedativo

seductive . . . . seductivo *(more commonly*
                                        "seductor(a)")

selective . . . . **selectivo**

sensitive . . . . sensitivo *(meaning "perceptive")*

speculative . . . . especulativo

subjective . . . . **subjetivo**

subjunctive . . . . subjuntivo

subversive. . . . . subversivo

successive. . . . . sucesivo

suggestive. . . . . sugestivo *(also used for "attractive")*

superlative . . . . superlativo

tentative . . . . tentativo

transitive. . . . . transitivo

unproductive . . . . improductivo

vegetative. . . . . vegetativo

votive. . . . . votivo

16A.

Una las palabras que están relacionadas o que son sinónimos.

1. creativo	pesimista
2. consecutivo	optimista
3. negativo	imaginativo
4. positivo	siguiente
5. competitivo	causa
6. productivo	ganador
7. motivo	eficiente

16B.

Escuche y lea el cuento. Responda las siguientes preguntas, usando oraciones completas.

Juan encuentra a Andalucía absolutamente fascinante. Había escuchado (he had heard) **muchas cosas <u>negativas</u> sobre Andalucía, pero él ve una región <u>creativa</u> y <u>productiva</u>. También Angélica tiene una impresión <u>positiva</u> de Andalucía. Antes de partir Juan quiere ir a buscar el pueblo** (the village) **donde nació su abuelo. "Un buen <u>motivo</u> para ir",** dice Angélica. Van a Jerez, un pueblo poco <u>activo</u> pero muy acogedor (welcoming). **Pasan dos días <u>consecutivos</u> allí.**

1. ¿Qué había escuchado Juan sobre Andalucía?

2. ¿Qué piensa Juan ahora sobre Andalucía?

3. ¿Qué impresión tiene Angélica de Andalucía?

4. ¿Cómo es el pueblo de Jerez?

5. ¿Cuántos días pasan allí?

Chapter 17

English words ending in "–ment" often correspond to "–mento" in Spanish.

Spanish words ending in "–mento" are usually masculine nouns. For example,

a monument = *un monumento*

ENGLISH . . . . SPANISH

All words and phrases in **bold** *are on* **Track 17** *of the accompanying audio.*

apartment . . . . **apartamento**
   "What a beautiful apartment." . . . **"¡Qué apartamento tan bonito!"**
argument . . . . argumento *(also used for "plot/story line")*
armament . . . . armamento

cement . . . . **cemento**
compartment . . . . compartimento
complement . . . . complemento
condiment . . . . condimento

department . . . . **departamento** *(also used for "apartment")*
   "I'm looking for   **"Busco el Departamento**
   the Spanish Department." . . . . **de Español".**
detriment . . . . detrimento
document . . . . **documento**

element . . . . **elemento**
excrement . . . . excremento
experiment . . . . experimento

ferment. . . . . fermento *(only a noun)*
filament . . . . filamento
firmament. . . . . firmamento
fragment . . . . **fragmento**

impediment. . . . . impedimento
implement. . . . . implemento
increment . . . . incremento
instrument . . . . **instrumento**

lament . . . . lamento
ligament. . . . . ligamento

microelement . . . . microelemento
moment . . . . **momento**
    "One moment, please." . . . . . **"Un momento, por favor".**
monument . . . . **monumento**

ornament . . . . **ornamento**

parliament . . . . parlamento
pavement . . . . pavimento
pigment . . . . pigmento

rudiment. . . . . rudimento

sacrament. . . . . sacramento
sediment. . . . . sedimento
segment . . . . **segmento**
supplement . . . . suplemento

temperament. . . . . temperamento
testament . . . . testamento
torment. . . . . tormento

Sometimes English words ending in "–ment" will correspond to "–miento" in Spanish. Following are seventeen (17) of the most commonly used words that follow this pattern:

commandment > mandamiento
comportment > comportamiento
discernment > discernimiento
enchantment > encantamiento
enrichment > enriquecimiento
entertainment > entretenimiento
equipment > equipamiento
establishment > establecimiento
movement > movimiento
presentiment > presentimiento
recruitment > reclutamiento
refinement > refinamiento
regiment > regimiento
requirement > requerimiento
resentment > resentimiento
sentiment > sentimiento
treatment > tratamiento

17A.

Una las palabras que están relacionadas o que son sinónimos.

1. instrumento	medicina
2. apartamento	papel
3. momento	renta
4. documento	instante
5. tratamiento	guitarra
6. segmento	héroes
7. monumento	parte

17B.

Escuche y lea el cuento. Responda las siguientes preguntas, usando oraciones completas.

En camino hacia el norte (on the way north) **el argumento era si ir a Córdoba o no. El tío de Angélica vive allá y tiene un apartamento para ellos. Él es profesor en el departamento de finanzas en la universidad en Córdoba. El problema es que él siempre tiene algún comentario sobre el comportamiento de ellos. Él es muy formal, y nunca da un halago** (compliment)**. Juan no quiere ir porque piensa que será un tormento. Angélica dice, "Vamos, Juan, hazme este favor** (do me this favor)**, y después vamos adonde tú quieras". Por un momento Juan quiere decir que no, pero al final dice, "Está bien, cariño, vamos a Córdoba".**

1. ¿Cuál es el argumento en camino hacia el norte?

2. ¿Dónde vive el tío de Angélica?

3. ¿Qué hace su tío?

4. ¿Por qué Juan no quiere ir a Córdoba?

5. Al final, ¿deciden ir a Córdoba o no?

Chapter 18 -or/-or

Many English words ending in "–or" have the same ending in Spanish.

Spanish words ending in "–or" are usually masculine nouns. For example,

a motor = *un motor*

ENGLISH . . . . SPANISH	

All words and phrases in **bold** are on **Track 18** of the accompanying audio.

accelerator . . . . acelerador

accumulator . . . . acumulador *(also used for "car battery")*

actor . . . . **actor**

    "He's a good actor." . . . . **"Es buen actor".**

adaptor . . . . adaptador

administrator. . . . . administrador

aggressor . . . . agresor

agitator . . . . agitador

alternator . . . . alternador

ambassador . . . . embajador

animator. . . . . animador *(also used for "presenter")*

anterior . . . . anterior

applicator. . . . . aplicador

ardor . . . . ardor

aspirator . . . . aspirador *(also used for "vacuum cleaner")*

assessor . . . . asesor *(meaning "consultant")*

auditor. . . . . auditor

author . . . . **autor**

aviator . . . . aviador

benefactor . . . . benefactor

calculator	calculador
calibrator	calibrador
candor	candor *(meaning "innocence")*
cantor	cantor
captivator	cautivador
carburator	carburador
censor	censor
clamor	clamor
co-editor	coeditor
collaborator	colaborador
collector	coleccionador
color	**color**
"What a nice color."	**"Qué color tan bonito".**
commentator	comentador
communicator	comunicador
competitor	competidor
condor	cóndor
conductor	conductor *(for music, use "director")*
confessor	confesor
connector	conectador
conquistador	conquistador
constructor	constructor
contaminator	contaminador
contributor	contribuidor
cooperator	cooperador
coordinator	coordinador
corrector	corrector
corruptor	corruptor
creator	**creador**
cultivator	cultivador
cursor	cursor
debtor	deudor
decorator	decorador
denominator	denominador

detonator	detonador
detractor	detractor
devastator	devastador
dictator	**dictador**
director	**director**
dishonor	deshonor
distributor	distribuidor
divisor	divisor
doctor	**doctor**
dolor	dolor *(meaning "pain")*
donor	donador
editor	editor
educator	educador
elector	elector
elevator	elevador
emperor	emperador
equator	ecuador
error	**error**
"It's a big error."	**"Es un gran error".**
excavator	excavador
exterior	**exterior**
exterminator	exterminador
extractor	extractor
facilitator	facilitador
factor	factor
favor	**favor**
fervor	fervor
fumigator	fumigador
furor	furor
generator	generador
gladiator	gladiador
governor	gobernador

honor	honor
horror	**horror**
humor	humor *(also used for "mood" and "temper")*
illuminator	iluminador
illustrator	ilustrador
imitator	imitador
impostor	impostor
improvisor	improvisador
incinerator	incinerador
indicator	indicador
inferior	**inferior** *(also used for "lower")*
initiator	iniciador
innovator	**innovador**
inspector	inspector
instigator	instigador
instructor	instructor
interceptor	interceptor
interior	**interior**
interlocutor	interlocutor
interrogator	interrogador
interruptor	interruptor *(also used for "electrical switch")*
inventor	**inventor**
"Thomas Edison was an inventor."	**"Thomas Edison fue un inventor".**
investigator	investigador
laminator	laminador
legislator	legislador
liberator	libertador
liquidator	liquidador
liquor	licor
major	mayor *(meaning "bigger" or "older")*

manipulator . . . . manipulador
matador . . . . matador
mediator. . . . . mediador
mentor . . . . mentor
minor . . . . menor *(also used for "smaller"*
                                        or "younger")
mitigator. . . . . mitigador
moderator . . . . moderador
monitor . . . . monitor
motor. . . . . **motor**
multicolor . . . . multicolor

narrator . . . . narrador
navigator . . . . navegador *(more commonly*
                                        "navegante")
negotiator. . . . . negociador

odor . . . . **olor** *(also used for "scent")*
operator. . . . . operador
oppressor . . . . opresor
orator. . . . . orador

pastor . . . . pastor
persecutor. . . . . perseguidor
possessor . . . . poseedor
posterior. . . . . posterior
preceptor . . . . preceptor
precursor . . . . precursor
predator. . . . . depredador
predecessor . . . . predecesor
processor . . . . procesador
procreator . . . . procreador
professor . . . . **profesor** *(also used for "teacher")*
projector . . . . proyector
propagator. . . . . propagador
protector . . . . **protector**

radiator . . . . radiador

rancor . . . . rencor

raptor . . . . raptor

reactor . . . . reactor

receptor . . . . receptor

rector . . . . rector

reflector . . . . reflector

refrigerator . . . . refrigerador

regulator . . . . regulador

renovator . . . . renovador

repressor . . . . represor

respirator . . . . respirador

resuscitator . . . . resucitador

rigor . . . . rigor

rotor . . . . rotor

rumor . . . . rumor *(also used for "murmur")*

savior . . . . salvador

sculptor . . . . escultor

sector . . . . sector

selector . . . . selector

semiconductor . . . . semiconductor

senator . . . . **senador**

sensor . . . . sensor

separator . . . . separador

simulator . . . . simulador

spectator . . . . espectador

speculator . . . . especulador

splendor . . . . esplendor

stupor . . . . estupor

successor . . . . sucesor

superior . . . . superior *(also used for "upper")*

supervisor . . . . supervisor

suppressor . . . . supresor

technicolor . . . . tecnicolor

tenor . . . . tenor

terminator . . . . terminador

terror . . . . **terror**

tractor . . . . tractor

traitor . . . . traidor

transgressor . . . . transgresor

transistor . . . . transistor

translator . . . . traductor

tremor . . . . temblor

tricolor . . . . tricolor

tumor . . . . **tumor**

    "It's a benign tumor." . . . . **"Es un tumor benigno".**

tutor . . . . tutor *(also used for "guardian")*

ulterior . . . . ulterior

valor . . . . valor

vapor . . . . **vapor**

vector . . . . vector

vendor . . . . vendedor

ventilator . . . . ventilador *(meaning "electric fan")*

violator . . . . violador *(also used for "rapist")*

vibrator . . . . vibrador

vigor . . . . vigor

18A.

Una las palabras que están relacionadas o que son sinónimos.

1. motor	gracias
2. color	afuera
3. favor	coche
4. terror	libro
5. autor	patente
6. inventor	horror
7. exterior	verde

18B.

Escuche y lea el cuento. Responda las siguientes preguntas, usando oraciones completas.

Apenas llegan a Córdoba, el tío les dice que habrá una fiesta en su casa esa noche. Angélica nota inmediatamente el <u>terror</u> en la cara de Juan. Cuando están sólos, Juan dice, "¡Qué <u>error</u> venir aquí! Hazme un <u>favor</u> y dime que no tengo que ir (I don't have to go) **a esa fiesta". Angélica ni siquiera responde** (doesn't even respond) **y Juan comprende que debe ir. La "fiesta" es muy difícil para Juan. Cada dos minutos, el tío dice, "Aquel hombre es <u>doctor</u>, aquel allá es <u>profesor</u>, el otro es <u>inventor</u>". Por un momentito Juan se interesa** (he's interested) **cuando el tío dice, "El <u>senador</u> va a venir con un <u>actor</u> muy famoso". Pero el <u>actor</u> no es famoso y el <u>senador</u> es muy, muy viejo.**

1. ¿Qué nota Angélica en la cara de Juan?

2. ¿Qué dice Juan sobre la decisión de ir a Córdoba?

3. ¿Qué dice Juan sobre la fiesta?

4. ¿El actor es famoso?

5. ¿El senador es joven?

English words ending in "–ory" generally correspond to "–orio" in Spanish.

Spanish words ending in "–orio" are usually adjectives or masculine nouns. For example,

> contradictory (adj.) = *contradictorio*
> laboratory (n.) = *el laboratorio*

ENGLISH. . . . . . . SPANISH

All words and phrases in **bold** are on **Track 19** of the accompanying audio.

accessory . . . . **accesorio**
  "She's buying an accessory." . . . **"Ella compra un accesorio"**.
accusatory . . . . acusatorio
ambulatory . . . . ambulatorio
anti-inflammatory . . . . antiinflammatorio

circulatory . . . . circulatorio
combinatory . . . . combinatorio
compensatory . . . . compensatorio
conservatory . . . . conservatorio
contradictory . . . . **contradictorio**
  "It's a contradictory response." . . . **"Es una respuesta contradictoria"**.
crematory . . . . crematorio

defamatory . . . . difamatorio
directory . . . . directorio
discriminatory . . . . discriminatorio
dormitory . . . . dormitorio

illusory . . . . ilusorio

inflammatory. . . . . inflamatorio
introductory . . . . introductorio

laboratory . . . . **laboratorio**
lavatory . . . . lavatorio

migratory . . . . migratorio

obligatory . . . . **obligatorio**
observatory . . . . observatorio
oratory. . . . . oratorio

peremptory. . . . . perentorio
predatory . . . . depredatorio
preparatory . . . . preparatorio
promissory . . . . promisorio
promontory. . . . . promontorio
provisory . . . . provisorio *(more commonly*
                                         "provisional")

purgatory. . . . . **purgatorio**
     "Dante wrote about   **"Dante escribió del**
     purgatory." . . . . **purgatorio".**

reformatory. . . . . reformatorio
repertory . . . . repertorio
repository. . . . . repositorio
respiratory . . . . respiratorio

satisfactory. . . . . satisfactorio
suppository. . . . . supositorio

territory . . . . **territorio**
transitory . . . . transitorio

unsatisfactory . . . . insatisfactorio

INSTANT Spanish Vocabulary Builder

19A.

Una las palabras que están relacionadas o que son sinónimos.

1. accesorio	zona
2. territorio	aretes
3. dormitorio	telescopio
4. laboratorio	insulto
5. observatorio	prólogo
6. derogatorio	experimento
7. introductorio	cama

19B.

Escuche y lea el cuento. Responda las siguientes preguntas, usando oraciones completas.

Juan está muy contento cuando finalmente parten de Córdoba hacia Sevilla. Dice, "Hubiera preferido (I'd have preferred) **un hostal".
Angélica admite que fue un <u>territorio</u> extraño. Juan dice, "Pero, ¿qué dices? ¡Fue peor que el <u>purgatorio</u>!" Angélica responde, "No tenías que** (you didn't have to) **venir, no era <u>obligatorio</u>". Juan se ríe de ese comentario <u>contradictorio</u> pero no responde. Juan dice, "Entonces me debes** (you owe me) **un favor, ¿verdad?" Angélica dice, "Veremos...".**

1. ¿Adónde van después de Córdoba?

2. ¿Qué hubiera preferido Juan?

3. Juan dice que la fiesta fue peor que ¿qué?

4. ¿Es verdad que su presencia (his presence) no era obligatoria?

5. ¿Responde Juan al último comentario contradictorio de Angélica?

Chapter 20

-OUS/-OSO

English words ending in "–ous" generally correspond to "–oso" in Spanish.

Spanish words ending in "–oso" are usually adjectives. For example,

a <u>generous</u> gift = *un regalo <u>generoso</u>*

ENGLISH . . . . SPANISH

All words and phrases in **bold** *are on* **Track 20** *of the accompanying audio.*

advantageous . . . . ventajoso
ambitious . . . . **ambicioso**
amorous . . . . amoroso
anxious . . . . ansioso

calamitous . . . . calamitoso
callous . . . . calloso
cancerous . . . . canceroso
capricious . . . . caprichoso
cavernous . . . . cavernoso
ceremonious . . . . ceremonioso
clamorous . . . . clamoroso
contagious . . . . contagioso
copious . . . . copioso
curious . . . . **curioso**

decorous . . . . decoroso
delicious . . . . **delicioso**
    "The food is delicious." . . . . . **"La comida es deliciosa"**.
desirous . . . . deseoso
disadvantageous . . . . desventajoso
disastrous . . . . **desastroso**

dubious . . . . dudoso

envious . . . . envidioso

fabulous . . . . fabuloso
famous . . . . famoso
fastidious . . . . fastidioso *(meaning "annoying")*
fibrous . . . . fibroso
furious . . . . **furioso**

gaseous . . . . gaseoso
gelatinous . . . . gelatinoso
generous . . . . **generoso**
    "She is very generous." . . . . . **"Ella es muy generosa".**
glamorous . . . . glamoroso
glorious . . . . glorioso
gracious . . . . gracioso *(meaning "funny")*

harmonious . . . . armonioso

ignominious . . . . ignominioso
impetuous . . . . impetuoso
incestuous . . . . incestuoso
indecorous . . . . indecoroso
industrious . . . . industrioso
ingenious . . . . ingenioso
insidious . . . . insidioso

jealous . . . . celoso
joyous . . . . jubiloso
judicious . . . . juicioso

laborious . . . . laborioso
litigious . . . . litigioso
luminous . . . . luminoso
luxurious . . . . lujoso

malicious . . . . malicioso
marvelous . . . . maravilloso
melodious . . . . melodioso
meticulous . . . . meticuloso
miraculous . . . . milagroso
monstrous . . . . monstruoso
mucous . . . . mucoso
mysterious . . . . **misterioso**

nebulous . . . . nebuloso
nervous . . . . **nervioso**
    "Are you nervous?" . . . . "**¿Estás nervioso?**"
numerous . . . . numeroso

obsequious . . . . obsequioso
odious . . . . odioso
onerous . . . . oneroso
ostentatious . . . . ostentoso

perilous . . . . peligroso
pernicious . . . . pernicioso
pious . . . . piadoso
pompous . . . . pomposo
populous . . . . populoso
porous . . . . poroso
portentous . . . . portentoso
precious . . . . **precioso**
prestigious . . . . **prestigioso**
presumptuous . . . . presuntuoso
pretentious . . . . pretencioso
prodigious . . . . prodigioso

rancorous . . . . rencoroso
religious . . . . **religioso**
rigorous . . . . riguroso
ruinous . . . . ruinoso

scabrous	escabroso
scandalous	**escandaloso**
scrupulous	escrupuloso
semiprecious	semiprecioso
sinuous	sinuoso
spacious	**espacioso**
studious	estudioso
sumptuous	suntuoso
superstitious	supersticioso
suspicious	sospechoso
tedious	tedioso
tempestuous	tempestuoso
tortuous	**tortuoso**
"The trip was tortuous."	**"El viaje fue tortuoso".**
tumultuous	tumultuoso
vaporous	vaporoso
vicious	vicioso *(meaning "depraved," or "addicted")*
victorious	victorioso
vigorous	vigoroso
virtuous	**virtuoso**
viscous	viscoso
voluminous	voluminoso
voluptuous	voluptuoso

20A.

Una las palabras que están relacionadas o que son sinónimos.

1. curioso	enojado
2. famoso	amplio
3. delicioso	suspenso
4. misterioso	sabroso
5. furioso	inquisitivo
6. precioso	diamante
7. espacioso	celebridad

20B.

Escuche y lea el cuento. Responda las siguientes preguntas, usando oraciones completas.

Después de la visita <u>desastrosa</u> a Córdoba, los dos viajeros están listos para un fin de semana <u>ambicioso</u> en Sevilla. Angélica sabe que este lugar (this place) **es <u>famoso</u> por los churros <u>deliciosos</u>, pero no sabe mucho más de la ciudad. Juan también está muy <u>curioso</u> por conocer a Sevilla. Su amigo le dijo** (told him) **que hay un aire <u>misterioso</u> allí. En la Universidad de Sevilla hay un programa <u>famoso</u> de lenguas extranjeras. Angélica dice, "Cualquiera que estudie** (whoever studies) **en el extranjero debe ser <u>ambicioso</u>". Están en un hotel muy <u>espacioso</u>, y se encuentran muy bien allí. Antes de partir para Toledo, Angélica dice, "Me gusta mucho Sevilla, pero no es un lugar <u>misterioso</u>, ¡tal vez tu amigo es un tipo <u>nervioso</u>!"**

1. ¿Qué tipo de fin de semana quieren pasar en Sevilla?

2. ¿Por qué es famosa Sevilla?

3. ¿Qué dijo el amigo de Juan sobre esta ciudad?

4. ¿Cuál es el programa famoso en la Universidad de Sevilla?

5. ¿Cómo es su hotel?

-sion/-sión

English words ending in "–sion" generally correspond to "–sión" in Spanish.

Spanish words ending in "–sión" are usually feminine nouns. For example,

an explosion = *una explosión*

ENGLISH . . . . SPANISH

All words and phrases in **bold** *are on* **Track 21** *of the accompanying audio.*

abrasion. . . . . abrasión
adhesion . . . . adhesión
admission. . . . . admisión
aggression . . . . agresión
allusion . . . . alusión
apprehension . . . . aprehensión
ascension . . . . ascensión
aversion . . . . aversión

circumcision . . . . circuncisión
cohesion. . . . . cohesión
collision . . . . **colisión**
    "There was a collision." . . . . . **"Hubo una colisión"**.
collusion. . . . . colusión
commission. . . . . comisión
compassion . . . . compasión
comprehension . . . . **comprensión**
compression . . . . compresión
compulsion . . . . compulsión
concession . . . . concesión
conclusion. . . . . **conclusión**
confession . . . . confesión

confusion	**confusión**
contusion	contusión
conversion	conversión
convulsion	convulsión
corrosion	corrosión
decision	**decisión**
decompression	descompresión
depression	depresión
diffusion	difusión
digression	digresión
dimension	**dimensión**
discussion	discusión *(meaning "argument")*
disillusion	desilusión *(also used for "disappointment")*
dispersion	dispersión
dissension	disensión
dissuasion	disuasión
diversion	diversión
division	**división**
effusion	efusión
emission	emisión
emulsion	emulsión
erosion	erosión
evasion	evasión *(also used for "escape")*
exclusion	exclusión
excursion	excursión
expansion	expansión
explosion	**explosión**
expression	**expresión**
"Another idiomatic expression!"	**"¡Otra expresión idiomática!"**
expulsion	expulsión
extension	extensión
extroversion	extroversión

INSTANT Spanish Vocabulary Builder

fission . . . . fisión

fusion . . . . fusión *(also used for "merger")*

hypertension . . . . hipertensión

illusion . . . . ilusión
immersion . . . . inmersión
implosion . . . . implosión
imprecision . . . . imprecisión
impression . . . . **impresión** *(also used for "printing")*
incision . . . . incisión
inclusion . . . . inclusión
incomprehension . . . . incomprensión
indecision . . . . indecisión
infusion . . . . infusión
intercession . . . . intercesión
intermission . . . . intermisión *(for shows/theater, use "entreacto")*
introversion . . . . introversión
intrusion . . . . intrusión
invasion . . . . invasión
inversion . . . . inversión

lesion . . . . lesión

mansion . . . . mansión
mission . . . . **misión**

obsession . . . . obsesión
occasion . . . . ocasión *(also used for "opportunity")*
occlusion . . . . oclusión
omission . . . . omisión
oppression . . . . opresión

passion . . . . **pasión**
"I have a passion for   **"Siento pasión por**
     Spanish." . . . . **el español".**

pension . . . . pensión *(also used for "small hotel")*

percussion . . . . percusión

persuasion . . . . persuasión

perversion . . . . perversión

possession . . . . posesión

precision. . . . . **precisión**

pretension. . . . . pretensión

prevision . . . . previsión

procession . . . . procesión

profession. . . . . **profesión**

profusion . . . . profusión

progression. . . . . progresión

propulsion . . . . propulsión

provision . . . . provisión

recession . . . . recesión

reclusion. . . . . reclusión

regression. . . . . regresión

remission . . . . remisión

repercussion . . . . repercusión

reprehension. . . . . reprensión

repression. . . . . represión

repulsion . . . . repulsión

reversion . . . . reversión

revision . . . . revisión

revulsion. . . . . revulsión *(only used in a medical context)*

secession . . . . secesión

session. . . . . **sesión**

subdivision . . . . subdivisión

submersion . . . . inmersión

submission . . . . sumisión

subversion . . . . subversión
succession . . . . sucesión
supervision . . . . supervisión
suppression. . . . . supresión
suspension . . . . suspensión

television . . . . **televisión**
   "Let's watch television." . . . . . **"Miremos la televisión"**.
tension . . . . **tensión**
transfusion . . . . transfusión
transgression. . . . . transgresión
transmission . . . . transmisión

version . . . . versión
vision . . . . **visión**

21A.

Una las palabras que están relacionadas o que son sinónimos.

1. confusión	caos
2. misión	bomba
3. televisión	antena
4. explosión	objetivo
5. pasión	ojo
6. precisión	exactitud
7. visión	amor

21B.

Escuche y lea el cuento. Responda las siguientes preguntas, usando oraciones completas.

Apenas llegan a Toledo, Angélica declara, "Tenemos una <u>misión</u> clara aquí en Toledo. Tú sabes que la cerámica es una <u>pasión</u> mía, ¿verdad? Tengo que encontrar (I must find) un plato de cerámica nuevo para mi colección". Juan dice, "Está bien, pero ¿tal vez lo podemos encontrar en La Coruña?" Angélica insiste, "¡NO! ¡Mi <u>decisión</u> es final! Quiero un plato de Toledo". Juan tiene la <u>impresión</u> de que Angélica no está bromeando (isn't kidding around), y él se dedica a la "<u>misión</u> del plato". Después de un almuerzo fabuloso en la plaza ellos comienzan la caza (the hunt). Había un poco de <u>confusión</u> con todas las callejuelas y callejones, pero al final hay una <u>conclusión</u> feliz— Angélica encuentra su plato.

1. ¿Cuál es la misión de Angélica?

2. ¿Por qué quiere eso?

3. ¿Qué dice Angélica de su decisión?

4. ¿Qué impresión tiene Juan de Angélica?

5. ¿Por qué había un poco de confusión?

-sis/-sis

English words ending in "–sis" often have the same ending in Spanish.

Spanish words ending in "–sis" are usually nouns. For example,

an analysis = *un análisis*

All words and phrases in
bold *are on* **Track 22** *of the
accompanying audio.*

ENGLISH. . . . . . . SPANISH

analysis . . . . **análisis**
antithesis . . . . antítesis

biogenesis . . . . biogénesis

catalysis . . . . catálisis
catharsis. . . . . catarsis
chassis . . . . chasís
cirrhosis . . . . cirrosis
crisis . . . . **crisis**

diagnosis . . . . diagnosis
dialysis. . . . . **diálisis**

electrolysis . . . . electrólisis
emphasis . . . . **énfasis**
    "You need more emphasis." . . . **"Necesitas más énfasis".**

fibrosis. . . . . fibrosis

genesis. . . . . **génesis**

halitosis . . . . halitosis
hydrolysis . . . . hidrólisis
hypnosis . . . . **hipnosis**
hypothesis . . . . **hipótesis**
   "What is your hypothesis?" . . . **"¿Cúal es tu hipótesis?"**

macroanalysis . . . . macroanálisis
metamorphosis . . . . **metamorfosis**
metastasis . . . . metástasis
microanalysis . . . . microanálisis
mononucleosis . . . . mononucleosis

narcosis . . . . narcosis
nemesis . . . . némesis
neurosis . . . . neurosis

oasis . . . . oasis
osmosis . . . . ósmosis
osteoporosis . . . . osteoporosis

paralysis . . . . parálisis
parenthesis . . . . paréntesis
photogenesis . . . . fotogénesis
photosynthesis . . . . fotosíntesis
prognosis . . . . prognosis
prosthesis . . . . prótesis
psoriasis . . . . psoriasis
psychoanalysis . . . . psicoanálisis
psychosis . . . . psicosis

sclerosis . . . . esclerosis
scoliosis . . . . escoliosis
self-analysis . . . . autoanálisis
synopsis . . . . sinopsis
synthesis . . . . síntesis

thesis . . . . **tesis**

   "Did he write his thesis?" . . . . **"¿Él escribió la tesis?"**

tuberculosis . . . . tuberculosis

22A.

Una las palabras que están relacionadas o que son sinónimos.

1. crisis	soñar
2. tuberculosis	enfermedad
3. énfasis	cambio
4. parálisis	dificultad
5. hipnosis	inmovilidad
6. metamorfosis	acento
7. análisis	estudio

22B.

Escuche y lea el cuento. Responda las siguientes preguntas, usando oraciones completas.

Destinación: ¡Madrid! Juan y Angélica ya conocen a (already know) **Madrid bastante bien. Entonces no ponen mucho énfasis en el giro turístico. Van a buscar, en cambio, a un primo de Juan que estudia en Madrid. Se llama Carlos y estudia economía. Escribe su tesis sobre la crisis financiera del tercer mundo** (of the Third World)**. Juan y Angélica cenan en casa de Carlos y escuchan mientras Carlos habla largo y tendido sobre su análisis de la crisis. Carlos dice, "Desafortunadamente, no tengo una hipótesis propia sobre como mejorar** (to improve) **la crisis, y sin esta hipótesis ¡no puedo hacer mi tesis!" Carlos pregunta a Juan, "¿Puedes ayudarme?" Juan responde, "Veremos...".**

1. ¿Por qué no ponen mucho énfasis en el giro turístico en Madrid?

2. ¿Sobre qué escribe la tesis Carlos?

3. ¿Carlos habla mucho sobre su análisis?

4. ¿Tiene Carlos una buena hipótesis para su tesis?

5. ¿Qué pregunta Carlos a Juan?

-tion/-ción

English words that end in "–tion" often correspond to "–ción" in Spanish.

Spanish words ending in "–ción" are usually feminine nouns. For example,

an operation = *una operación*

ENGLISH . . . . SPANISH

All words and phrases in **bold** are on **Track 23** of the accompanying audio.

abbreviation . . . . abreviación *(meaning "a shortening")*
abdication . . . . abdicación
aberration . . . . aberración
abolition. . . . . abolición
abomination . . . . abominación
absolution. . . . . absolución
absorption . . . . absorción
abstention. . . . . abstención
abstraction . . . . abstracción
acceleration . . . . aceleración
acclamation . . . . aclamación
accommodation. . . . . acomodación *(more commonly "alojamiento," for lodging)*

accreditation. . . . . acreditación
acculturation . . . . aculturación
accumulation . . . . acumulación
accusation . . . . acusación
acquisition . . . . adquisición
action. . . . . **acción** *(also used for "stock share")*
   "There's not a lot of action." . . . **"No hay mucha acción"**.
activation . . . . activación

actualization . . . . actualización

adaptation . . . . adaptación

addiction . . . . adicción

addition . . . . adición

administration . . . . administración

admiration . . . . admiración

admonition . . . . admonición

adoption . . . . adopción

adoration . . . . adoración

adulation . . . . adulación

adulteration . . . . adulteración

affiliation . . . . afiliación

affirmation . . . . afirmación

affliction . . . . aflicción

agitation . . . . agitación

alienation . . . . alienación

alliteration . . . . aliteración

alteration . . . . alteración

ambition . . . . **ambición**

   "They have ambition." . . . . . . **"Tienen ambición".**

Americanization . . . . americanización

amputation . . . . amputación

animation . . . . animación

annotation . . . . anotación

anticipation . . . . anticipación

apparition . . . . aparición

application . . . . aplicación *(for "application form,"*
                                       use "solicitud")

appreciation . . . . apreciación

approbation . . . . aprobación

approximation . . . . aproximación

aspiration . . . . aspiración

assimilation . . . . asimilación

association . . . . asociación

attention . . . . **atención** *(also used for*
                                  "attention please!")

attenuation . . . . atenuación

attraction . . . . atracción

attribution . . . . atribución

audition . . . . audición

authentication . . . . autenticación

authorization . . . . autorización

automation . . . . automatización

aviation . . . . aviación *(also used for "air force")*

benediction . . . . bendición

cancellation . . . . cancelación

capitalization . . . . capitalización

celebration . . . . **celebración**

   "It's a big celebration." . . . . . **"Es una gran celebración"**.

centralization . . . . centralización

certification . . . . certificación

circulation . . . . circulación

citation . . . . citación

civilization . . . . civilización

classification . . . . clasificación

coaction . . . . coacción

coalition . . . . coalición

codification . . . . codificación

cognition . . . . cognición

cohabitation . . . . cohabitación

collaboration . . . . colaboración

collection . . . . colección

colonization . . . . colonización

coloration . . . . coloración

combination . . . . combinación

commemoration . . . . conmemoración

commiseration . . . . conmiseración

commotion . . . . conmoción

communication . . . . comunicación

compensation . . . . compensación

competition. . . . . competición

compilation. . . . . compilación

complication . . . . complicación

composition . . . . composición

concentration . . . . concentración

conception . . . . concepción

condensation . . . . condensación

condition . . . . **condición**

conduction . . . . conducción *(also used for "the act of guiding")*

confection. . . . . confección *(meaning "the making of")*

confederation . . . . confederación

confirmation . . . . confirmación

confiscation . . . . confiscación

conformation. . . . . conformación

confrontation. . . . . confrontación

congregation . . . . congregación

conjugation. . . . . conjugación

conjunction. . . . . conjunción

connotation. . . . . connotación

conservation . . . . conservación

consideration . . . . consideración

consolation. . . . . consolación

consolidation . . . . consolidación

constellation . . . . constelación

consternation . . . . consternación

constipation . . . . constipación *(meaning "head congestion")*

constitution . . . . constitución

constriction . . . . constricción

construction . . . . construcción

consummation. . . . . consumación

contamination . . . . contaminación *(also used for "pollution")*

contemplation . . . . contemplación

contention. . . . . contención *(meaning "retention")*

continuation . . . . continuación

contraction	contracción
contradiction	contradicción
contribution	contribución
contrition	contrición
convention	convención
conversation	**conversación**
conviction	convicción
cooperation	cooperación
coordination	**coordinación**
coproduction	coproducción
coronation	coronación
corporation	corporación
correction	corrección
correlation	correlación
corruption	corrupción
creation	creación
cremation	cremación
crystallization	cristalización
culmination	culminación
cumulation	acumulación

decapitation	decapitación
deceleration	desaceleración
decentralization	descentralización
deception	decepción *(meaning "disappointment")*
declamation	declamación
declaration	declaración
declination	declinación
decomposition	descomposición
decoration	decoración
dedication	dedicación
deduction	deducción
defamation	difamación
definition	**definición**
deflation	deflación *(only used in an economic context)*

deforestation . . . . desforestación

deformation . . . . deformación

degeneration . . . . degeneración

degradation . . . . degradación

dehumanization . . . . deshumanización

dehydration . . . . deshidratación

delegation . . . . delegación

deliberation . . . . deliberación

delimitation . . . . delimitación

demarcation . . . . demarcación

demolition . . . . demolición

demonstration . . . . demostración

denomination . . . . denominación

deportation . . . . deportación

depravation . . . . depravación

depreciation . . . . depreciación

description . . . . descripción

desertion . . . . deserción

desolation . . . . desolación

desperation . . . . desesperación

destabilization . . . . desestabilización

destination . . . . destinación

destitution . . . . destitución *(meaning "dismissal")*

destruction . . . . **destrucción**

detention . . . . detención

determination . . . . determinación

devastation . . . . devastación

deviation . . . . desviación

devotion . . . . devoción

diction . . . . dicción

differentiation . . . . diferenciación

digestion . . . . digestión

direction . . . . **dirección** *(also used for "street address")*

discretion . . . . discreción

discrimination . . . . discriminación

INSTANT Spanish Vocabulary Builder

disfunction . . . . disfunción
disintegration . . . . desintegración
disorganization . . . . desorganización
disorientation . . . . desorientación
disposition . . . . disposición
disproportion . . . . desproporción
disqualification . . . . descalificación
dissection . . . . disección
dissertation . . . . disertación
distillation . . . . destilación
distinction . . . . distinción
distraction . . . . distracción
distribution . . . . distribución
diversification . . . . diversificación
documentation . . . . documentación
domination . . . . dominación
donation . . . . donación
dramatization . . . . dramatización
duplication . . . . duplicación
duration . . . . duración

edition . . . . **edición**
   "It's a new edition." . . . . **"Es una nueva edición".**
education . . . . educación *(also used for "manners")*
ejection . . . . eyección *(more commonly "expulsión")*
elaboration . . . . elaboración
election . . . . elección
electrocution . . . . electrocución
elevation . . . . elevación
elimination . . . . eliminación
elocution . . . . elocución
emancipation . . . . emancipación
embarcation . . . . embarcación *(meaning "boat")*
emigration . . . . emigración
emotion . . . . **emoción**
emulation . . . . emulación

enunciation . . . . enunciación

equation . . . . ecuación

erection . . . . erección

erudition . . . . erudición

eruption . . . . erupción

evaluation . . . . evaluación

evaporation . . . . evaporación

evolution . . . . evolución

exaggeration . . . . **exageración**

examination . . . . examinación *(more commonly "examen")*

exasperation . . . . exasperación

excavation . . . . excavación

exception . . . . excepción

exclamation . . . . exclamación

excretion . . . . excreción

execution . . . . ejecución

exhibition . . . . exhibición

exhortation . . . . exhortación

expedition . . . . expedición

exploration . . . . exploración

exportation . . . . exportación

exposition . . . . exposición

extinction . . . . extinción

extraction . . . . extracción

extradition . . . . extradición

exultation . . . . exultación

fabrication . . . . fabricación *(meaning "manufacturing")*

falsification . . . . falsificación

federation . . . . federación

fermentation . . . . fermentación

fertilization . . . . fertilización

fiction . . . . ficción

filtration . . . . filtración

finalization . . . . finalización

fixation . . . . fijación

fluctuation. . . . . fluctuación

formation . . . . formación *(also used for*
"training")

formulation . . . . formulación

fossilization. . . . . fosilización

foundation . . . . **fundación**

fraction . . . . fracción

fragmentation . . . . fragmentación

friction . . . . fricción

fruition . . . . fruición

frustration . . . . frustración

fumigation . . . . fumigación

function . . . . función

generalization. . . . . generalización

generation . . . . **generación**

"Every generation changes.". . . **"Cada generación cambia"**.

germination . . . . germinación

gestation . . . . gestación

globalization. . . . . globalización

glorification . . . . glorificación

graduation . . . . graduación

gratification . . . . gratificación *(also used for "tip")*

gravitation . . . . gravitación

habitation. . . . . habitación *(meaning "bedroom")*

hallucination. . . . . alucinación

humiliation . . . . humillación

identification. . . . . identificación

ignition. . . . . ignición

illumination. . . . . iluminación

illustration. . . . . ilustración

imagination . . . . imaginación

imitation . . . . **imitación**

"It's a horrible imitation!" . . . . **"¡Es una mala imitación!"**

immigration . . . . inmigración

imperfection . . . . imperfección

implication . . . . implicación

importation . . . . importación

improvisation . . . . improvisación

inaction . . . . inacción

inauguration . . . . inauguración

incarnation . . . . encarnación

incineration . . . . incineración

inclination . . . . inclinación

incrimination . . . . incriminación

incubation . . . . incubación

indignation . . . . indignación

indiscretion . . . . indiscreción

induction . . . . inducción

infatuation . . . . infatuación *(meaning "vanity")*

infection . . . . infección

infiltration . . . . infiltración

inflamation . . . . inflamación

inflation . . . . inflación

information . . . . **información**

inhibition . . . . inhibición

initiation . . . . iniciación

injection . . . . inyección

innovation . . . . innovación

inquisition . . . . inquisición

inscription . . . . inscripción *(also used for "enrollment,"*
"registration")

insemination . . . . inseminación

insertion . . . . inserción

inspection . . . . inspección

inspiration . . . . inspiración

installation . . . . instalación

institution . . . . institución

instruction . . . . instrucción
insurrection . . . . insurrección
integration . . . . integración
intensification . . . . intensificación
intention . . . . **intención**
interaction . . . . interacción
interception . . . . interceptación
interpretation . . . . interpretación
interrogation . . . . interrogación
interruption . . . . interrupción
intersection . . . . intersección
intervention . . . . intervención *(also used for "surgery")*
intimidation . . . . intimidación
intonation . . . . entonación
intoxication . . . . intoxicación *(meaning "poisoning")*
introduction . . . . introducción
introspection . . . . introspección
intuition . . . . intuición
inundation . . . . inundación
invention . . . . **invención**
investigation . . . . investigación
invitation . . . . invitación
irrigation . . . . irrigación
irritation . . . . irritación *(also used for "rash")*

justification . . . . justificación
juxtaposition . . . . yuxtaposición

lamination . . . . laminación
legalization . . . . legalización
legislation . . . . legislación
levitation . . . . levitación
liberation . . . . liberación
limitation . . . . limitación
liposuction . . . . liposucción
liquidation . . . . liquidación

litigation . . . . litigación
location . . . . localización
locomotion . . . . locomoción
lotion . . . . **loción**
    "We don't have any more lotion." . . . **"No tenemos más loción".**
lubrication . . . . lubricación

malformation. . . . . malformación
malnutrition. . . . . malnutrición
manifestation . . . . manifestación *(also used for*
                                 "public demonstration")
manipulation. . . . . manipulación
masturbation. . . . . masturbación
maturation . . . . maduración
medication . . . . medicación
meditation . . . . meditación
memorization . . . . memorización
menstruation . . . . menstruación
mention . . . . mención
migration . . . . migración
mitigation . . . . mitigación
moderation. . . . . moderación
modification . . . . modificación
modulation . . . . modulación
monopolization . . . . monopolización
motion . . . . moción *(meaning "proposal")*
motivation. . . . . motivación
multiplication . . . . multiplicación
mutation . . . . mutación

narration . . . . narración
nation . . . . **nación**
navigation . . . . navegación
negation. . . . . negación
negotiation . . . . negociación
nomination . . . . nominación

notation . . . . notación
notion . . . . noción
nutrition . . . . nutrición

objection . . . . objeción
obligation. . . . . obligación
observation. . . . . observación
obstruction . . . . obstrucción
occupation . . . . ocupación
operation . . . . **operación**
   "She needs an operation.". . . . **"Ella necesita una operación"**.
opposition . . . . oposición
option . . . . opción
oration. . . . . oración
organization . . . . organización
orientation . . . . orientación
ovulation . . . . ovulación
oxidation . . . . oxidación

pagination . . . . paginación
palpitation . . . . palpitación
participation . . . . participación
partition . . . . partición
penetration . . . . penetración
perception . . . . percepción
perfection. . . . . perfección
perforation . . . . perforación
perpetuation . . . . perpetuación
persecution . . . . persecución
personalization . . . . personalización
personification . . . . personificación
petition. . . . . petición
pollution. . . . . polución
population . . . . **población**
portion. . . . . porción

position . . . . **posición** *(for employment, use "puesto")*

"What is his/her position?" . . . **"¿Cúal es su posición?"**

postproduction . . . . posproducción

postulation . . . . postulación

potion . . . . poción

precaution . . . . precaución

precipitation . . . . precipitación

precondition . . . . precondición

predestination . . . . predestinación

prediction . . . . predicción

predilection . . . . predilección

predisposition . . . . predisposición

premeditation . . . . premeditación

premonition . . . . premonición

preoccupation . . . . **preocupación**

preparation . . . . preparación

preposition . . . . preposición

prescription . . . . prescripción

presentation . . . . presentación

preservation . . . . preservación

presumption . . . . presunción

prevention . . . . prevención

privation . . . . privación

privatization . . . . privatización

proclamation . . . . proclamación

procreation . . . . procreación

production . . . . producción

prohibition . . . . prohibición

projection . . . . proyección

proliferation . . . . proliferación

promotion . . . . promoción

pronunciation . . . . pronunciación

proportion . . . . proporción

proposition . . . . proposición

prostitution . . . . prostitución

protection . . . . protección
provocation . . . . provocación
publication . . . . publicación
punctuation. . . . . puntuación
purification . . . . purificación

qualification . . . . cualificación
quantification . . . . cuantificación

radiation . . . . radiación
ramification . . . . ramificación
ration. . . . . ración
reaction . . . . **reacción**
reactivation. . . . . reactivación
realization . . . . realización *(meaning "completion")*
reception . . . . recepción
recommendation . . . . recomendación
recollection. . . . . recolección *(meaning "gathering")*
reconciliation . . . . reconciliación
recreation. . . . . recreación
recrimination. . . . . recriminación
recuperation . . . . recuperación
reduction . . . . reducción
reelection . . . . reelección
reevaluation . . . . reevaluación
refraction . . . . refracción
refrigeration . . . . refrigeración
regulation. . . . . regulación
rehabilitation. . . . . rehabilitación
reincarnation . . . . reencarnación
relation . . . . relación
relaxation. . . . . relajación
renovation . . . . renovación
reorganization . . . . reorganización
reparation . . . . reparación
repetition . . . . repetición

reproduction . . . . reproducción

reputation. . . . . **reputación**

   "He has a good reputation." . . . **"Él tiene una buena reputación".**

reservation . . . . reservación

resignation . . . . resignación *(meaning "yielding";*
*   "job resignation" is*
*   "dimisión")*

resolution . . . . resolución

respiration . . . . respiración

restitution . . . . restitución

restoration . . . . restauración

restriction . . . . restricción

resurrection. . . . . resurrección

retention. . . . . retención

retraction . . . . retracción

retribution . . . . retribución

revelation . . . . revelación

revolution . . . . **revolución**

rotation . . . . rotación

salvation . . . . salvación

sanction . . . . sanción

satisfaction . . . . **satisfacción**

   "It gives me a lot of satisfaction." . . . **"Me da mucha satisfacción".**

saturation . . . . saturación

secretion. . . . . secreción

section . . . . sección

sedation. . . . . sedación

sedition . . . . sedición

seduction . . . . seducción

segmentation . . . . segmentación

segregation . . . . segregación

selection. . . . . selección

self-destruction. . . . . autodestrucción

sensation . . . . sensación

separation . . . . separación

simplification	simplificación
simulation	simulación
situation	**situación**
solution	**solución**
sophistication	sofisticación
specialization	especialización
specification	especificación
speculation	especulación
stabilization	estabilización
station	**estación**
sterilization	esterilización
stimulation	estimulación *(more commonly "estímulo")*
stipulation	estipulación
sublimation	sublimación
subordination	subordinación
substitution	sustitución
subtraction	sustracción
superstition	superstición
supposition	suposición
synchronization	sincronización
temptation	tentación
termination	terminación
tradition	**tradición**
"It's a long tradition."	**"Es una larga tradición".**
transaction	transacción
transcription	transcripción
transformation	transformación
transition	transición
trepidation	trepidación
tribulation	tribulación
unification	unificación

vacation	vacación
vacillation	vacilación
validation	validación
variation	variación
vegetation	vegetación
veneration	veneración
ventilation	ventilación
verification	verificación
vibration	vibración
vindication	vindicación
violation	violación
visualization	visualización
vocalization	vocalización
vocation	vocación

23A.

Una las palabras que están relacionadas o que son sinónimos.

1.	información		sentimiento
2.	dirección		a la derecha
3.	estación		fiesta
4.	nación		noticias
5.	emoción		país
6.	solución		tren
7.	celebración		resultado

23B.

Escuche y lea el cuento. Responda las siguientes preguntas, usando oraciones completas.

En la <u>estación</u> de Salamanca, Juan y Angélica ven un anuncio (a sign) para una gran <u>celebración</u> en la plaza principal para esa noche. Leen la <u>información</u> y comprenden que esta fiesta será grande. Angélica no quiere ir porque no se siente bien (she doesn't feel well). Juan dice, "Así me pagas el favor". Angélica ve que la <u>reacción</u> de Juan es fuerte y ella dice, "Está bien, vamos". Juan dice, "Pero qué <u>situación</u> perfecta para conocer esta bella ciudad y su cocina". La <u>reacción</u> de Angélica es más sobria (subdued). Ella dice, "Sí, nos encontramos en una buena <u>posición</u> aquí". Al final de la fiesta Juan está más tranquilo. Él dice, "Angélica, comí y bebí demasiado, debo irme a dormir".

1. ¿Dónde ven el anuncio para la celebración?

2. ¿Cómo será esta fiesta?

3. ¿Por qué es importante la celebración para Juan?

4. ¿Cómo es la reacción de Angélica?

5. Al final de la fiesta, ¿en qué condición se encuentra Juan?

-ty/-dad

Many English words that end in "–ty" correspond to "–dad" in Spanish.

Spanish words ending in "–dad" are usually feminine nouns. For example,

the responsibility = *la responsabilidad*

Chapter 24

ENGLISH . . . . SPANISH

All words and phrases in **bold** *are on* **Track 24** *of the accompanying audio.*

ability . . . . habilidad
abnormality . . . . anormalidad
acceptability . . . . aceptabilidad
accessibility . . . . accesibilidad
activity . . . . **actividad**
actuality . . . . actualidad *(meaning "current events")*
adaptability . . . . adaptabilidad
admissibility . . . . admisibilidad
adversity . . . . adversidad
affinity . . . . afinidad
aggressivity . . . . agresividad
agility . . . . agilidad
alacrity. . . . . alacridad
ambiguity . . . . ambigüedad
amenity . . . . amenidad
amorality . . . . amoralidad
animosity . . . . animosidad
annuity. . . . . anualidad
antiquity . . . . antigüedad
anxiety. . . . . **ansiedad**
    "You have too much anxiety." . . . **"Tienes demasiada ansiedad"**.
applicability . . . . aplicabilidad

artificiality	artificialidad
atrocity	atrocidad
austerity	austeridad
authenticity	autenticidad
authority	autoridad
banality	banalidad
barbarity	barbaridad
bisexuality	bisexualidad
brevity	brevedad
brutality	brutalidad
calamity	calamidad
capacity	capacidad
cavity	cavidad *(for teeth, use "caries")*
celebrity	**celebridad**
"Paul Newman is a celebrity."	**"Paul Newman es una celebridad".**
centrality	centralidad
charity	caridad
chastity	castidad
Christianity	Cristiandad
city	ciudad
civility	civilidad
clarity	claridad
collectivity	colectividad
commodity	comodidad *(meaning "comfort," "convenience")*
communicability	comunicabilidad
community	**comunidad**
compatibility	compatibilidad
complexity	complejidad
complicity	complicidad
conductivity	conductividad
conformity	conformidad
continuity	continuidad

cordiality . . . . cordialidad
corruptibility . . . . corruptibilidad
creativity . . . . **creatividad**
credibility . . . . credibilidad
cruelty . . . . crueldad
culpability . . . . culpabilidad
curiosity . . . . **curiosidad**

debility . . . . debilidad
deformity . . . . deformidad
density . . . . densidad
difficulty . . . . **dificultad**
dignity . . . . dignidad
discontinuity . . . . discontinuidad
dishonesty . . . . deshonestidad
disparity . . . . disparidad
diversity . . . . diversidad
divinity . . . . divinidad
divisibility . . . . divisibilidad
domesticity . . . . domesticidad
duality . . . . dualidad
duplicity . . . . duplicidad
durability . . . . durabilidad

elasticity . . . . elasticidad
electricity . . . . **electricidad**
   "There is no electricity." . . . . . **"No hay electricidad"**.
eligibility . . . . elegibilidad
enormity . . . . enormidad
entity . . . . entidad
equality . . . . igualdad
equanimity . . . . ecuanimidad
equity . . . . equidad
eternity . . . . eternidad
eventuality . . . . eventualidad
exclusivity . . . . exclusividad

expressivity . . . . expresividad

extremity . . . . extremidad

facility . . . . facilidad *(meaning "talent" or "ease")*

faculty . . . . *facultad *(only used for "university department," "right," or "ability")*

fallibility . . . . falibilidad

falsity . . . . falsedad

familiarity . . . . familiaridad

fatality . . . . fatalidad *(also used for "misfortune," "disaster")*

felicity . . . . felicidad

femininity . . . . feminidad

ferocity . . . . ferocidad

fertility . . . . fertilidad

festivity . . . . festividad

fidelity . . . . fidelidad

finality . . . . finalidad *(meaning "goal," "objective")*

flexibility . . . . **flexibilidad**
   "It's important   **"Es importante**
   to have flexibility." . . . . **tener flexibilidad".**

formality . . . . formalidad

fragility . . . . fragilidad

fraternity . . . . fraternidad

frugality . . . . frugalidad

functionality . . . . funcionalidad

futility . . . . futilidad

generality . . . . generalidad

generosity . . . . **generosidad**

governability . . . . gobernabilidad

gratuity . . . . gratuidad *(meaning "free," "no charge")*

gravity . . . . gravedad

heterosexuality . . . . heterosexualidad
hilarity . . . . hilaridad
homosexuality . . . . homosexualidad
honesty . . . . honestidad
hospitality . . . . hospitalidad
hostility . . . . hostilidad
humanity . . . . humanidad
humidity . . . . humedad
humility . . . . humildad
hyperactivity . . . . hiperactividad

identity . . . . **identidad**
illegality . . . . ilegalidad
illegibility . . . . ilegibilidad
immensity . . . . inmensidad
immortality . . . . inmortalidad
immunity . . . . inmunidad
impartiality . . . . imparcialidad
impassivity . . . . impasibilidad
impermeability . . . . impermeabilidad
impiety . . . . impiedad
impossibility . . . . **imposibilidad**
improbability . . . . improbabilidad
impropriety . . . . impropiedad
inactivity . . . . inactividad
incapacity . . . . incapacidad
incompatibility . . . . incompatibilidad
inconformity . . . . inconformidad
incredulity . . . . incredulidad
indignity . . . . indignidad
individuality . . . . individualidad
inequality . . . . desigualdad
inevitability . . . . inevitabilidad
infallibility . . . . infalibilidad
inferiority . . . . inferioridad
infertility . . . . infertilidad

infidelity . . . . infidelidad
infinity . . . . infinidad
infirmity . . . . enfermedad
inflexibility . . . . inflexibilidad
informality . . . . informalidad
ingenuity . . . . ingenuidad *(meaning "innocence,"*
"naiveté")

iniquity. . . . . iniquidad
insecurity . . . . inseguridad
insensitivity . . . . insensibilidad
insincerity. . . . . insinceridad
instability . . . . inestabilidad
integrity . . . . integridad
intensity . . . . **intensidad**
intolerability . . . . intolerabilidad
invariability. . . . . invariabilidad
invisibility . . . . invisibilidad
invulnerability . . . . invulnerabilidad
irrationality . . . . irracionalidad
irregularity . . . . irregularidad
irresponsibility. . . . . irresponsabilidad

legality. . . . . legalidad
legibility. . . . . legibilidad
liberty . . . . ***libertad**
"Here's the Statue   **"La Estatua de la Libertad**
of Liberty." . . . . **está aquí".**
locality. . . . . localidad
longevity . . . . longevidad
loyalty . . . . *lealtad

magnanimity. . . . . magnanimidad
majesty . . . . *majestad
malleability. . . . . maleabilidad
marginality . . . . marginalidad
masculinity . . . . masculinidad

maternity . . . . maternidad
mediocrity . . . . mediocridad
mentality . . . . mentalidad
mobility . . . . movilidad
modality . . . . modalidad
modernity . . . . modernidad
monstrosity . . . . monstruosidad
morality . . . . moralidad
mortality . . . . mortalidad
multiplicity . . . . multiplicidad
mutability . . . . mutabilidad
mutuality . . . . mutualidad
municipality . . . . municipalidad

Nativity . . . . Navidad *(meaning "Christmas")*
necessity . . . . **necesidad**
negativity . . . . negatividad
neutrality . . . . neutralidad
normality . . . . normalidad
notoriety . . . . notoriedad
novelty . . . . novedad

obesity . . . . obesidad
objectivity . . . . objetividad
obscenity . . . . obscenidad
obscurity . . . . oscuridad *(meaning "darkness")*
opportunity . . . . **oportunidad**
originality . . . . originalidad

parity . . . . paridad
partiality . . . . parcialidad
particularity . . . . particularidad
passivity . . . . pasividad
paternity . . . . paternidad
peculiarity . . . . peculiaridad

penalty	penalidad *(meaning "suffering," "hardship")*
permeability	permeabilidad
permissibility	permisibilidad
perpetuity	perpetuidad
perplexity	perplejidad
personality	**personalidad**
perversity	perversidad
piety	piedad *(meaning "pity")*
plasticity	plasticidad
plurality	pluralidad
polarity	polaridad
popularity	popularidad
possibility	**posibilidad**

"There's a lot of possibility." . . . **"Hay mucha posibilidad"**.

posterity	posteridad
priority	prioridad
probability	probabilidad
productivity	productividad
profundity	profundidad
promiscuity	promiscuidad
property	propiedad
prosperity	prosperidad
proximity	proximidad
puberty	pubertad
publicity	publicidad *(also used for "advertising")*
punctuality	puntualidad
quality	**calidad**
quantity	**cantidad**
rationality	racionalidad
reality	realidad
regularity	regularidad
relativity	relatividad
respectability	respetabilidad

responsibility. . . . . **responsabilidad**
   "Whose responsibility is it?". . . **"¿De quién es la**
                                               responsabilidad?"

-ty/-dad

sanity. . . . . sanidad *(meaning "general health")*
security. . . . . seguridad
selectivity . . . . selectividad
senility . . . . senilidad
sensibility . . . . sensibilidad
sensitivity . . . . sensibilidad
sensuality . . . . sensualidad
serenity . . . . serenidad
severity. . . . . severidad
sexuality. . . . . sexualidad
similarity. . . . . similaridad
simplicity . . . . simplicidad
sincerity . . . . sinceridad
singularity. . . . . singularidad
sobriety . . . . sobriedad
society . . . . sociedad
solidarity . . . . solidaridad
solubility. . . . . solubilidad
speciality . . . . **especialidad**
spirituality. . . . . espiritualidad
spontaneity. . . . . espontaneidad
stability . . . . estabilidad
sterility . . . . esterilidad
subjectivity . . . . subjetividad
superficiality . . . . superficialidad
superiority . . . . superioridad

temerity . . . . temeridad
temporality . . . . temporalidad
tenacity . . . . tenacidad
tonality. . . . . tonalidad
totality . . . . totalidad

tranquility	tranquilidad
trinity	trinidad
triviality	trivialidad
ubiquity	ubicuidad
uniformity	uniformidad
unity	unidad
universality	universalidad
university	**universidad**

    "It's a good university." . . . . . **"Es una buena universidad".**

utility	utilidad *(meaning "usefulness")*
vanity	vanidad
variability	variabilidad
variety	variedad
velocity	velocidad
verity	verdad *(meaning "truth")*
versatility	versatilidad
viability	viabilidad
vicinity	vecindad
virginity	virginidad
virility	virilidad
virtuality	virtualidad
viscosity	viscosidad
visibility	**visibilidad**
vitality	vitalidad
vivacity	vivacidad
volatility	volatilidad
voracity	voracidad
vulgarity	vulgaridad
vulnerability	vulnerabilidad

*these words end in –tad, not –dad

24A.

Una las palabras que están relacionadas o que son sinónimos.

1. calidad		excelencia
2. creatividad		luz
3. personalidad		abundancia
4. universidad		arte
5. cantidad		carácter
6. electricidad		infinito
7. eternidad		profesora

24B.

Escuche y lea el cuento. Responda las siguientes preguntas, usando oraciones completas.

La última ciudad para Juan y Angélica es La Coruña. Angélica está muy entusiasmada; dice que La Coruña es una <u>ciudad</u> con mucha <u>creatividad</u> y <u>actividad</u>. Juan dice que le gusta mucho la <u>personalidad</u> de este lugar. No tienen mucha <u>dificultad</u> en andar por las calles y puentes (bridges) **de la <u>ciudad</u>. La Coruña es una bella <u>comunidad</u> y ellos permanecen allí** (they stay there) **por cuatro días. Un día Angélica cree ver** (she thinks she sees) **una <u>celebridad</u>: Antonio Banderas. Pero Juan dice que es una <u>imposibilidad</u>, porque Banderas está filmando una película en Suiza. Antes de partir a casa, Juan dice, "Angélica, tengo una pregunta, podemos vivir aquí en La Coruña algún día?" Angélica responde, "Sí, sí, hay muchas <u>posibilidades</u> para nosotros aquí. Veremos…".**

1. ¿Qué dice Angélica de La Coruña?

2. ¿Qué le gusta a Juan de esta ciudad?

3. ¿Tienen dificultad en andar por La Coruña?

4. ¿Angélica ve a una celebridad?

5. ¿Quiere Angélica vivir en La Coruña algún día? ¿Qué dice?

ANSWER KEY

1A.

1. animal: gato
2. personal: privado
3. artificial: sintético
4. crucial: importante
5. ideal: perfecto
6. legal: contrato
7. final: terminar

1B.

1. Juan y Angélica son de Bilbao.
2. Juan quiere hacer un viaje internacional.
3. Angélica quiere hacer un viaje nacional.
4. Juan dice que la idea de Angélica no es original.
5. Según Juan, el tío de Angélica es demasiado formal y tradicional.

2A.

1. fragancia: perfume
2. distancia: lejos
3. perseverancia: constancia
4. tolerancia: paciencia
5. arrogancia: soberbia
6. ambulancia: hospital
7. importancia: significado

2B.

1. Juan habla de la importancia de no gastar mucho.
2. Juan no tiene mucha tolerancia hacia el mundo "chic".
3. La perseverancia será necesaria.
4. Sí, Angélica entiende la importancia de no gastar mucho dinero.
5. Juan responde, "Veremos".

3A.

1. ignorante: desconocedor
2. elegante: fino
3. importante: esencial
4. elefante: animal
5. arrogante: pretencioso
6. flagrante: evidente
7. restaurante: cafetería

3B.

1. Van a Barcelona
2. Angélica piensa que la gente de Barcelona es arrogante.
3. Juan dice que el modo de vestir de la gente de Barcelona es muy elegante.
4. Juan dice que la historia de Barcelona es muy importante.
5. El restaurante de Andrés se llama El Elefante Rojo.

4A.

1. cardiovascular: corazón
2. regular: constante
3. singular: único
4. circular: redondo
5. similar: parecido
6. dólar: moneda
7. nuclear: atómico

4B.

1. Van a una lección de italiano mientras están en Barcelona.
2. Andrés estudia italiano porque el italiano es muy popular en Ibiza, y quiere trabajar en Ibiza.
3. El profesor habla de muchos verbos irregulares.
4. Los tres amigos hablan de la diferencia entre el singular y el plural en el italiano.
5. No, Angélica piensa que el italiano es muy irregular (difícil).

5A.

1. aniversario: cumpleaños
2. salario: dinero
3. necesario: vital
4. vocabulario: palabras
5. itinerario: ruta
6. ordinario: común
7. contrario: opuesto

5B.

1. El itinerario de Juan y Angélica es muy intenso en Barcelona.
2. Angélica quiere comprar un diario.
3. Angélica escribe mucho/todo/cada detalle en su diario.
4. Juan dice que el ritmo es extraordinario.
5. Según Juan, no es necesario escribir cada detalle en el diario.

6A.

1. flexible: elástico
2. terrible: horrible
3. probable: posible
4. estable: seguro
5. inflexible: rígido
6. miserable: infeliz
7. adorable: bonito

6B.

1. Después de Barcelona van a Valencia.
2. Angélica piensa que Juan es muy irresponsable.
3. Juan dice que Angélica es inflexible.
4. Angélica piensa que es (bastante) improbable que regresen a Valencia
   algún día.
5. Al final, Angélica pregunta si será posible comprar los boletos en
   Valencia.

7A.

1. correcto: bien
2. perfecto: ideal
3. incorrecto: mal
4. dialecto: idioma
5. acto: teatro
6. aspecto: parte
7. insecto: mosca

7B.

1. Tomaron el tren directo de Barcelona a Valencia.
2. Angélica piensa que no es el lugar correcto porque no comprende nada.
3. Angélica no comprende el español en Valencia porque hay un acento fuerte.
4. El contacto de Juan en Valencia se llama Alfonso.
5. La salsa de Alfonso estuvo perfecta.

8A.

1. paciencia: esperar
2. conferencia: reunión
3. residencia: casa
4. diferencia: distinción
5. violencia: guerra
6. evidencia: prueba
7. independencia: liberación

8B.

1. Alfonso dice que él y su novia van al baile mañana por la noche.
2. Según Angélica la persistencia y diligencia ayudan.
3. Juan piensa que el baile será una buena experiencia.
4. A Juan el baile le causa indiferencia.
5. Juan pide disculpas por su impaciencia.

9A.

1. permanente: fijo
2. reciente: nuevo
3. diferente: distinto
4. presidente: jefe
5. evidente: obvio
6. residente: habitante
7. presente: actual

9B.

1. Angélica recibe un mensaje urgente.
2. Diego es el presidente de una compañia médica.
3. Angélica dice que su primo es diferente (inteligente/un médico competente).
4. Según Angélica, Diego es muy inteligente.
5. Al final Juan dice, "Está bien, veremos".

10A.

1. biología: vida
2. radiología: rayos X
3. tecnología: computadora
4. trilogía: tres
5. estrategia: plan
6. cronología: historia
7. geología: tierra

10B.

1. Diego tiene mucha energía.
2. Los muchachos no tienen alergia al café.
3. Diego habla de nuevas tecnologías.
4. Juan nunca ha estudiado radiología.
5. Angélica no estudia psicología.

11A.

1. pragmático: práctico
2. tráfico: carros
3. auténtico: verdadero
4. específico: detalles
5. electrónico: estéreo
6. clásico: intemporal
7. romántico: amoroso

11B.

1. Hay mucho tráfico.
2. Angélica dice que el tren es mejor porque no es muy romántico pasar las vacaciones dentro de un carro.
3. Van a algunos museos artísticos.
4. Alicante es mágico por la noche.
5. Alicante es una ciudad fantástica.

12A.

1. típico: usual
2. idéntico: igual
3. práctico: pragmático
4. biográfico: personal
5. diabólico: demoníaco
6. clínico: médico
7. crítico: importante

12B.

1. Juan quiere permanacer en Alicante.
2. Angélica quiere viajar de una manera lógica.
3. Sí, Angélica es siempre práctica.
4. Van a la Costa del Sol.
5. Angélica dice, "Tu también quieres ir a la Costa del Sol, ¿verdad?"

13A.

1. rápido: veloz
2. tímido: introvertido
3. estúpido: idiota
4. ácido: limón
5. frígido: helado
6. árido: seco
7. espléndido: maravilloso

13B.

1. Angélica dice que es un plan estúpido.
2. Juan piensa que es un plan (idea) espléndido.
3. Hace calor (muy húmedo) durante el viaje.
4. Angélica le compra un poco de antiácido para Juan cuando él se siente mal.
5. El farmacéutico dice que debe beber mucho líquido y no comer comida ácida.

14A.

1. turismo: vacaciones
2. comunismo: Karl Marx
3. patriotismo: nación
4. atletismo: olímpico
5. terrorismo: bomba
6. optimismo: positivo
7. criticismo: comentario

14B.

1. Sí, hay mucho turismo en la Costa del Sol.
2. El fascismo comenzó durante los años treinta.
3. Angélica lee sobre la influencia del comunismo y del socialismo en España.
4. Ellos hablan sobre el patriotismo español.
5. Al final Juan dice, "¡Tomemos un helado!"

15A.

1. artista: cantante
2. dentista: diente
3. turista: pasaporte
4. pesimista: negativo
5. idealista: positivo
6. finalista: campeón
7. capitalista: dinero

15B.

1. El muchacho es dentista.
2. Sí, los nuevos amigos de Juan y Angélica viajan a menudo.
3. Angélica tiene una lista de preguntas.
4. El dentista es pesimista y es realista.
5. La artista es optimista y es idealista.

16A.

1. creativo: imaginativo
2. consecutivo: siguiente
3. negativo: pesimista
4. positivo: optimista
5. competitivo: ganador
6. productivo: eficiente
7. motivo: causa

16B.

1. Juan había escuchado muchas cosas negativas sobre Andalucía.
2. Juan piensa que (ve) Andalucía es absolutamente fascinante.
3. Angélica tiene una impresión positiva de Andalucía.
4. El pueblo de Jerez es poco activo pero muy acogedor.
5. Pasan dos días consecutivos allí.

17A.

1. instrumento: guitarra

2. apartamento: renta

3. momento: instante

4. documento: papel

5. tratamiento: medicina

6. segmento: parte

7. monumento: héroes

17B.

1. El argumento en camino hacia el norte es si ir a Córdoba o no.

2. El tío de Angélica vive en Córdoba.

3. Su tío es profesor.

4. Juan no quiere ir a Córdoba porque el tío de Angélica siempre tiene algún comentario sobre el compartamiento de ellos (él es muy formal y nunca da un halago).

5. Sí, al final, deciden ir a Córdoba.

18A.

1. motor: coche

2. color: verde

3. favor: gracias

4. terror: horror

5. autor: libro

6. inventor: patente

7. exterior: afuera

18B.

1. Angélica nota el terror en la cara de Juan.

2. Juan dice, "¡Qué error venir aquí!" sobre la decisión de ir a Córdoba.

3. Juan dice, "Dime que no debo ir a esa fiesta".

4. No, el actor no es famoso.

5. No, el senador es muy, muy viejo.

19A.

1. accesorio: aretes
2. territorio: zona
3. dormitorio: cama
4. laboratorio: experimento
5. observatorio: telescopio
6. derogatorio: insulto
7. introductorio: prólogo

19B.

1. Después de Córdoba van a Sevilla.
2. Juan hubiera preferido un hostal.
3. Juan dice que la fiesta fue peor que el purgatorio.
4. No, no es verdad que su presencia no era obligatoria.
5. No, Juan no responde al último comentario contradictorio de Angélica.

20A.

1. curioso: inquisitivo
2. famoso: celebridad
3. delicioso: sabroso
4. misterioso: suspenso
5. furioso: enojado
6. precioso: diamante
7. espacioso: amplio

20B.

1. Quieren pasar un fin de semana ambicioso en Sevilla.
2. Sevilla es famosa por los churros deliciosos.
3. El amigo de Juan le dijo que hay un aire misterioso allí.
4. En la Universidad de Sevilla hay un programa famoso de lenguas extranjeras.
5. Su hotel es muy espacioso.

21A.

1. confusión: caos
2. misión: objetivo
3. televisión: antena
4. explosión: bomba
5. pasión: amor
6. precisión: exactitud
7. visión: ojo

21B.

1. La misión de Angélica es encontrar un plato de cerámica.
2. Quiere el plato para su colección.
3. Angélica dice que su decisión es final.
4. Juan tiene la impresión de que Angélica no está bromeando.
5. Había un poco de confusión con todas las callejuelas y callejones.

22A.

1. crisis: dificultad
2. tuberculosis: enfermedad
3. énfasis: acento
4. parálisis: inmovilidad
5. hipnosis: soñar
6. metamorfosis: cambio
7. análisis: estudio

22B.

1. No ponen mucho énfasis en el giro turístico porque ya conocen Madrid bastante bien.
2. Carlos escribe la tesis sobre la crisis financiera del tercer mundo.
3. Sí, Carlos habla largo y tendido sobre su análisis.
4. No, Carlos no tiene una buena hipótesis para su tesis.
5. Carlos pregunta a Juan, "¿Puedes ayudarme?"

23A.

1. información: noticias
2. dirección: a la derecha
3. estación: tren
4. nación: país
5. emoción: sentimiento
6. solución: resultado
7. celebración: fiesta

23B.

1. Ven el anuncio para la celebración en la estación de Salamanca.
2. Esta fiesta será grande.
3. La celebración es importante para Juan porque es la situación perfecta
   para conocer Salamanca y su cocina.
4. La reacción de Angélica es más sobria.
5. Al final de la fiesta Juan está mas tranquilo.

24A.

1. calidad: excelencia
2. creatividad: arte
3. personalidad: carácter
4. universidad: profesora
5. cantidad: abundancia
6. electricidad: luz
7. eternidad: infinito

24B.

1. Angélica dice que La Coruña es una ciudad con mucha creatividad y
   actividad.
2. A Juan le gusta la personalidad de esta ciudad.
3. No, no tienen dificultad en andar por La Coruña.
4. Angélica cree ver a una celebridad.
5. Angélica dice, "Sí, hay muchas posibilidades para nosostros aquí… veremos".

AUDIO TRACK LIST

	English suffix	Spanish suffix
Track 1 (3:36)	–al	–al
Track 2 (2:14)	–ance	–ancia
Track 3 (2:41)	–ant	–ante
Track 4 (1:58)	–ar	–ar
Track 5 (2:36)	–ary	–ario
Track 6 (3:58)	–ble	–ble
Track 7 (2:13)	–ct	–cto
Track 8 (3:16)	–ence	–encia
Track 9 (3:01)	–ent	–ente
Track 10 (2:45)	–gy	–gía
Track 11 (4:21)	–ic	–ico
Track 12 (2:23)	–ical	–ico
Track 13 (1:46)	–id	–ido
Track 14 (3:04)	–ism	–ismo
Track 15 (3:16)	–ist	–ista
Track 16 (3:19)	–ive	–ivo
Track 17 (2:20)	–ment	–mento
Track 18 (3:18)	–or	–or
Track 19 (1:50)	–ory	–orio
Track 20 (2:48)	–ous	–oso
Track 21 (3:03)	–sion	–sión
Track 22 (2:13)	–sis	–sis
Track 23 (5:05)	–tion	–ción
Track 24 (3:57)	–ty	–dad
Track 25 (1:18)	Pronunciation Guide	

CPSIA information can be obtained
at www.ICGtesting.com
Printed in the USA
LVOW13s0918160618
580664LV00004B/1/P